Infotech

English for computer users

Fourth Edition

Teacher's Book

CAMBRIDGE
UNIVERSITY PRESS

Santiago Remacha Esteras

CAMBRIDGE UNIVERSITY PRESS
Cambridge, New York, Melbourne, Madrid, Cape Town,
Singapore, São Paulo, Delhi, Tokyo, Mexico City

Cambridge University Press
The Edinburgh Building, Cambridge CB2 8RU, UK

www.cambridge.org
Information on this title: www.cambridge.org/9780521703000

First published 2008
5th printing 2011

Printed in the United Kingdom at the University Press, Cambridge

A catalogue record for this publication is available from the British Library

ISBN 978-0-521-703000 Teacher's Book
ISBN 978-0-521-702997 Student's Book
ISBN 978-0-521-703017 CD (audio)

Acknowledgements
The author gratefully acknowledges the help of Nick Robinson in preparing this work for publication.
The publishers would like to thank eMC Design and Ruth Carim.

1 *Who is* Infotech *for?*

Infotech is an intermediate-level English course for students of computer science and technical English in secondary schools, universities and technical colleges. It aims to help these students to develop a wide variety of language skills and to acquire a knowledge of computers *in English*.

Infotech is also suitable for in-house training programmes, and for institutions where English has become a requisite for working with computers. This book is intended to help professionals using computers (e.g. engineers and desktop publishers) to understand a wide range of texts about ICT technologies.

Infotech does not require a specialist knowledge of computers, but it is advisable for teachers to understand the basic concepts and terminology of each unit. These are explained either in the unit texts or in the Teacher's Book (see Teacher's notes or Technical help sections).

2 *What does* Infotech *consist of?*

The Student's Book contains:
- a Map of the Book;
- 30 teaching units organized into eight modules (each unit provides an average of two hours of work);
- an appendix with a sample Curriculum Vitae;
- a list of irregular verbs;
- a glossary of technical terms;
- a list of acronyms and abbreviations.

The Teacher's Book contains:
- unit planning sheets with practical teaching suggestions; teachers can also use these sheets to make notes about optional materials, learning difficulties and evaluation;
- the answer key;
- audio scripts for the CD listening material;
- technical help where it is required;
- eight tests covering the eight modules of the book; this test material covers vocabulary, grammar, reading and writing skills and can be used to assess your students' progress.

3 *Organization*

The material in *Infotech* is organized into 'thematic' modules, which cover a wide variety of topics and styles of presentation; it is based on skills development and communicative tasks.

Each module consists of three to five units based on the same theme. The first page of each module sets the theme and provides the learning objectives. Most of the units follow a similar pattern:
- A 'pre-task' to make the texts more accessible and prepare the students for the main task.
- A main task which focuses on a particular skill.

- Language work and vocabulary exercises. The purpose of these 'enabling activities' is to prepare students for freer practice.
- A follow-up task. The aim of this is to provide students with more opportunities for speaking or writing.

Although the overall framework of each unit is largely the same, the variety of tasks makes each unit unique.

The book presents the topics in gradual development, from computer essentials to more sophisticated issues such as networks and future trends, so we recommend that the units are studied in sequential order. This will help SS understand basic hardware and software components and then proceed to more complex matters like internet security, web design and wireless communications. However, another possibility is to study only those units that your students are interested in. For example, you may want to focus on particular topics, such as buying a computer, the Internet, or video games.

4 Skills development

Infotech lays particular emphasis on developing receptive skills – that is, reading and listening – although these skills are supported by speaking and writing activities.

- The **reading** texts are mostly authentic or adapted from original sources – specialist magazines, computer programs, reference manuals and websites. The tasks are designed to develop a variety of reading strategies, such as skimming, scanning, matching texts to pictures, etc. Text analysis is also a relevant feature of this book: students have to look for information, find reference signals, identify cohesion devices, or distinguish facts and opinions.
- The **listening** passages include conversations (e.g. buying a computer), interviews, online tutorials, podcasts, lectures, descriptions of hardware and software, etc. It can be helpful to start the listening tasks with a pre-listening activity, such as pre-teaching vocabulary, 'brainstorming' the topic, etc.
- The **speaking** tasks develop oral skills through quizzes, role plays, discussions, information-gap and problem solving activities.
- The approach to **writing** is based on two assumptions: (i) writing is an interactive process where the writer tries to communicate something to a real or imaginary reader; (ii) the organization of ideas is as important as grammatical accuracy. Consequently, the students are encouraged to write complete, coherent texts. The writing tasks include describing objects and diagrams, summarizing texts, writing essays with pros and cons, making predictions, writing posts for online forums, writing emails, faxes and letters, etc.

5 Grammar and vocabulary

The **Language work** tasks revise major language points necessary at this level. The **HELP boxes** in the units are designed as a resource which can be used as part of classroom teaching or outside the classroom. The language work concentrates on those grammatical constructions which are typical of technical English (passive forms, classifying structures, imperatives, modal verbs, comparatives and superlatives, discourse markers, etc.). Grammar exercises are contextualized and arise from the linguistic forms that appear in the oral or written texts. Sometimes students have to work out the grammar for themselves or compare with their mother tongue.

Infotech lays special emphasis on **vocabulary** acquisition. Below are a few tips about how to deal with it.

- Explain the difference between *active* and *passive* vocabulary. Some students are not conscious of this distinction and are very anxious about their lack of active vocabulary. Active vocabulary refers to those lexical items that the student is able to use appropriately in oral or written communication. Passive vocabulary refers to those items that can be recognized and understood during the process of listening and reading. Passive vocabulary is much easier to acquire than active vocabulary at any stage in the learning process.

- Tell your students that they do not need to understand every word in a text and encourage them to guess the meaning from context – the surrounding words and the situation. When students meet unknown words, it can also be useful to work out what part of speech they are – nouns, verbs, adjectives, etc. Word building exercises and the study of word formation processes (affixation, conversion and compounding) will help students to develop and extend their vocabulary.

- Explain the importance of learning word combinations, often called *collocations*. A collocation is a pair or group of words that are often used together. For example, we say *attach a file*, *make a phone call* (not *enclose a file*, *do a phone call*). Students need to learn collocations in order to sound more natural in English.

- Draw students' attention to the Glossary for help with acronyms and technical terms.

- Train students to use their dictionaries properly. Students should be able to understand the pronunciation guidance, the layout of entries, abbreviations, etc. They can visit the Cambridge dictionary website at www.dictionary.cambridge.org or an online computer dictionary on the Web, such as www.webopedia.com.

- Encourage students to use a notebook or a file on disk to write down important words and grammar points. Some students may also like to have an 'internet scrapbook', where they can paste the best things from the Web.

6 *Online activities*

The *Infotech* website at www.cambridge.org/elt/ict provides students with more opportunities to develop their knowledge and language skills online. The site contains an interactive PDF worksheet for each of the 30 units, which revises and consolidates vocabulary and grammar from the unit. Additionally, at the end of each module, students are invited to visit the *Infotech* website for an online task. These 'web quests' have been designed to encourage students to use the Web in English to carry out tasks related to the topics of each module. Each task comes with full teacher's notes.

The website is regularly updated to reflect advances in computer technology, and also includes new reading activities, a blog, a word of the week and podcasts. The site is also related to *Professional English in Use ICT*, a vocabulary book by Elena Marco Fabré and Santiago Remacha Esteras, published by Cambridge University Press.

1 Computers today

Learning objectives

In this module, you will:

- talk and write about computer applications in everyday life.
- study the basic structure of a computer system.
- study the differences between certain types of computer.
- learn how to classify computer devices.
- learn about the structure and functions of the CPU.
- learn how to distinguish between RAM and ROM.
- learn about how memory is measured.
- learn and use relative pronouns.
- learn how to enquire about computers in a shop.
- learn how to understand the technical specs of different computers.

Living in a digital age

Topics

Different uses of computers

The magic of computers

Learning objectives

To talk and write about computer applications in everyday life

Language

Grammar: Verb-noun collocations

Vocabulary: Computers in education, banks, offices, airports, libraries, entertainment, Formula 1 cars, factories, etc.

Basic terms: *digital, data, word processor, monitor, online, download, store*

Skills

Listening: Listening for specific information in short descriptions

Speaking: Discussing what computers can do in particular areas

Reading: Matching texts to pictures

Deciding where removed sentences should go in a text

Writing: Summarizing a discussion

Plan

Teacher's activities	Students' activities	Comments
Module page You may want to point out the learning objectives for your SS.	SS familiarize themselves with the topics and objectives of the Module.	
1 The digital age **A** Draw SS attention to the pictures. Then ask them to match each picture to a caption. **B** and **C** Ask SS to discuss how computers are used in the situations illustrated by the pictures. Then tell them to read the text to find out if they are correct. **D** and **E** Encourage SS to guess the meaning of unknown words from the context. **F** You may like to write some key language on the board: *Computers are used to …* *They can help us store/make calculations.* You can also write SS' answers on the board.	**A** SS match the captions to the pictures. **B** and **C** In pairs, SS discuss how computers are used in the situations illustrated by the pictures. They then read the text to check their answers. **D** SS guess the meaning of the words from context; they decide whether the words are nouns, verbs or adjectives. **E** SS match the words with the correct meanings. **F** SS discuss the questions, in pairs or as a whole class.	This first unit is deliberately less technical than the others. It is meant to be a gentle introduction to the book.

2 Language work: collocations 1 **A** Refer SS to the HELP box, explaining what collocations are and giving more examples if necessary. **B** Monitor the task, helping where needed.	**A** and **B** SS look at the HELP box and do exercises A and B individually. Then they check the answers in class feedback.	A collocation is a pair or group of words that are often used together. For example, we say *make phone calls*, not *do phone calls*. Collocations are very common in ICT language. SS need to learn them in order to sound natural in English.
3 Computers at work **A** Play track 2 of the CD, pausing after each speaker. **B** Play the CD again. You may like to draw the table on the board.	**A** SS listen and complete the middle column of the table. Then they compare answers with a partner. **B** SS listen again and complete the table.	You may like to give SS a copy of the audio script.
4 The magic of computers **A** and **B** Monitor the activities, helping with any vocabulary problems.	**A** SS read the text *The magic of computers* and decide where the removed sentences should go in the article. SS then answer the questions in **B**.	
5 Other applications **A** Encourage SS to spot the collocations in the *Useful language* box and to use them in their discussions. Monitor the discussions, helping where needed. **B** Give help with the summaries if necessary. Ask each group to appoint a spokesperson to give an oral report to the class.	**A** Each group discusses the use of computers in one of the four areas, using words and phrases from the *Useful language* box. **B** SS write a short presentation summarizing their discussion. One person from each group then presents the group's ideas to the class.	Weaker SS may find this task a little difficult. Draw their attention to the *Useful language* box for help.

Evaluation of the unit:

Answer key

1 The digital age

A

1b 2a 3d 4c

B

Open task

C

SS check answers to B

D

1 v
2 n
3 adj or adv (used as an adverb in this text)
4 v or n (used as a verb in this text)

5 adj
6 adj
7 n or v (used as a verb in this text)
8 adj
9 n or v (used as a noun in this text)
10 n

E

a7   b1   c8   d9   e5   f3   g10   h6   i2   j4

F

Open task

2 Language work: collocations 1

A

1d   2e   3c   4b   5a

B

1 access the Internet
2 transfer money
3 make calls
4 give presentations
5 do research
6 store information
7 send texts

3 Computers at work

A and **B**

Speaker	Job	What they use computers for
1	composer	To record what he plays on the keyboard; to get different sounds from the synthesizers
2	secretary	To write memos, letters and faxes; to communicate with other offices by email
3	electrical engineer	To design electrical installations and lighting systems; to make drawings; to keep records (of tests)
4	librarian	To catalogue and record the books, newspapers or DVDs that users borrow; to assist visitors in the use of hardware and software; to help people find specific information

4 The magic of computers

A

a2   b5   c4   d1   e3

B

1 Telephones, calculators, the car's electronic ignition, the timer in the microwave, the programmer inside the TV set
2 Hardware and software
3 Bills, customers' lists, accounts, inventories, letters, memos, legal documents, etc.
4 Because it enables you to interact with other computers and with people around the world.

5 Other applications

A

Possible answers

Entertainment: People use computers to play all kinds of computer games: chess, adventure games, simulation games, etc. Fortunately, entertainment software means more than just computer games. There are specialized programs for downloading, composing and playing music. PCs can combine sound, text and animated images and allow users to make video clips, watch DVDs and TV, and listen to the radio. Multimedia applications allow users to produce slide shows, retouch photographs, etc. Optical discs make encyclopedias and books available on computer.

Formula 1: Computers are used to design and build racing cars and test virtual models. Computers help engineers to design the car body and the mechanical parts. During races, a lot of microprocessors control the electronic components of the car and monitor the engine speed, temperature and other vital information.

Factories and industrial processes: Computers are used to control machinery, robots, production lines, lists of products, etc. By using computer-aided manufacturing software, engineers can simulate and test designs before parts are actually produced.

School/University: Students can use computers to help with their studies by accessing the Internet and searching the Web. A PC can also be used for enrolling online, doing exercises online and preparing presentations, as well as writing documents.

B

Open task

Audio script

Speaker 1

I write music mainly for videos and plays. I work on a keyboard connected to a computer. I use the computer in *two* ways, really: first of all, to record, or store, what I play on the keyboard. Secondly, the computer controls the sounds I can make with the different synthesizers I have here. I can use it to get different kinds of sound from the synthesizers. The computer is the link between the keyboard, which I play, and the synthesizers, which produce the sounds.

Speaker 2

I use my computer to do the usual office things, like writing memos, letters, faxes and so on, but the thing I find most useful is email. We're an international company, and we have offices all over the world. We're linked up to all of them by email. With email I can communicate with the offices around the world very efficiently. It's really changed my life.

Speaker 3

Well, I use computers for almost every aspect of my job. I use them to design electrical installations and lighting systems. For example, a program will tell you how much lighting you need for a particular room, or how much cable you need, and it'll show where the cable should go. I also use the computer to make drawings and to keep records. We have to test our installations every five years, and that information is stored on computer, too.

Speaker 4

I use computers to catalogue and classify all the materials received in the library, and record all the books, newspapers, DVDs, etc. that users borrow. I also assist customers and visitors in the use of IT hardware and software, including online databases and CD-ROMs. I help people with their enquiries, for example if children or elderly people need to find some specific information, either in our online library catalogue or on the Internet. I'm also in charge of other library services, such as printing and fax machines.

Computer essentials

Topic

The elements of a computer system

Learning objectives

To understand the basic structure of a computer system

To recognize the differences between these types of computer: mainframe, desktop PC, laptop, tablet PC and PDA

To classify computer devices

To use basic IT vocabulary

Language

Grammar: Classifying expressions

Vocabulary: Basic terminology: *hardware, software, input, output, CPU, main memory, peripherals, storage devices, disk drives, input devices, output devices, monitor, printer, mouse, keyboard, mainframe, desktop, laptop, notebook, tablet PC, PDA, modem (or router), camera, DVD, USB port*

Skills

Listening: Understanding the gist of a lecture about types of computer system

Speaking: Describing one's own computer and components

Describing a diagram using classifying expressions

Reading: Understanding specific information about the elements of a computer system

Matching slogans with computer elements

Writing: Writing an email describing the benefits of tablet PCs in the classroom or laptops in business

Plan

Teacher's activities	Students' activities	Comments
1 Computer hardware **A** Encourage SS to talk about the computer they have at home, school or work. After SS discuss the questions in pairs, elicit SS' answers in class feedback; this will allow you to see the level and range of technical vocabulary they already have. **B** You may want to write the labels on the board, as they are not printed on the page itself. **C** Ask SS to guess which computer element each slogan refers to. Tell them to try after reading the first clue; if they can't guess it, then they can use the second clue. **D** Monitor the activity, helping where needed.	**A** In pairs, SS discuss the questions. **B** SS label the elements of the computer system in the diagram. **C** SS read the slogans and try to guess which element they refer to. **D** SS then find words in the slogans that correspond to the given definitions.	

2 What is a computer?

A and **B**

Monitor the activities, checking any problems with technical terms. You may wish to give SS a few tips on how to deal with vocabulary (see Introduction, page 6).

In class feedback, ask for evidence from the text. This will help you assess SS' reading comprehension level.

A SS read the text and then explain the diagram in their own words.

B SS match the words with the definitions. They can use the Glossary, if necessary.

You may need to help SS with the following technical aspects: *hardware* in contrast to *software* (see Glossary); *input* in contrast to *output* (see the diagram on page 8 of the Student's Book).

3 Different types of computer

A Play track 3 of the CD.

B Play the CD again, pausing after each paragraph. Play the CD a third time without pausing.

A SS listen and label the pictures.

B SS then listen again, mark *True* or *False*, and then correct the false sentences.

SS should be able to differentiate between different types of computer: *mainframes*, *desktop PCs* (kept on a desk), *laptops* (sometimes held on one's lap), *tablet PCs,* and *PDAs* (or palmtops, held in one's hand).

4 Language work: classifying

A Refer SS to the HELP box, providing more examples if necessary.

B Monitor the activity, helping where needed.

A SS use suitable classifying expressions to complete the sentences.

B SS then describe a diagram about peripherals using classifying expressions, making reference to their own computer devices.

5 Benefits of laptops and tablet PCs

If your SS are studying at school or college, then set the first task. If your SS are currently working, then set the second task. You could set these tasks for homework.

SS write an email to their boss or their teacher, explaining the benefits of using laptops in business, or tablet PCs at school.

Some schools are now using tablet PCs or mobile computers in classrooms as part of the teaching/learning process.

Evaluation of the unit:

Answer key

1 Computer hardware

A

Open task

B

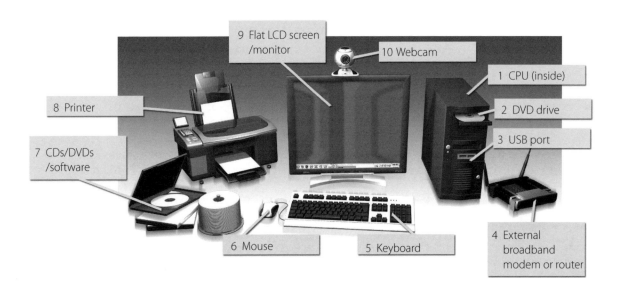

9 Flat LCD screen /monitor

10 Webcam

1 CPU (inside)

2 DVD drive

3 USB port

8 Printer

7 CDs/DVDs /software

6 Mouse

5 Keyboard

4 External broadband modem or router

C

1 mouse
2 screen/monitor
3 DVD drive (or hard drive)
4 CPU
5 printer

D

1 click
2 sharp
3 back up
4 range
5 displays

2 What is a computer?

A

Open task

B

1c   2f   3g   4h   5b   6d   7i   8e   9a

3 Different types of computer

A

a desktop PC
b tablet PC
c laptop
d mainframe
e PDA

B

1 False – A mainframe computer is more powerful than a PC
2 True
3 True
4 False – A laptop is portable
5 False – Laptops can be as powerful as desktop PCs
6 True
7 True
8 False – A PDA allows you to surf the Web

4 Language work: classifying

A

1 consists of
2 can be divided into / are classified into
3 includes / is a type of
4 There are two types/classes

B

Possible answer

Peripherals are often divided into three categories: input, output and storage devices.

Input devices include the keyboard, the mouse, scanners, cameras, etc. For example, I have a digital camera with 6.1 megapixel resolution. I take pictures and download them to the computer via a USB port.

Output devices include the monitor and the printer. I have a 17″ flat LCD screen and an inkjet printer.

There are three basic types of storage media: magnetic, optical and Flash memory. I have a hard drive with a capacity of 250GB, a DVD Rewritable drive that supports all types of CDs and DVDs, and a USB pen drive, which I use to share texts, music and video clips with friends.

5

Open task

Audio script

… as I'll explain to you now, computers can be divided into five main types, depending on their size and power. These are: mainframes, desktop PCs, laptops, tablet PCs and personal digital assistants, or PDAs.

Mainframes are the largest and most powerful computers. The basic configuration of a mainframe consists of a central system which processes immense amounts of data very quickly. This central system provides information and computing facilities for hundreds of terminals connected together in a network. Mainframes are used for large-scale computing purposes in banks, universities and big companies.

PCs, or personal computers, carry out their processing on a single microchip. They are usually classified by size and portability. A desktop PC is designed to be placed on your desk. It is used as a home computer or as a workstation for group work. Typical examples are the IBM PC and the Apple Macintosh.

A laptop is a portable computer that has a flat LCD screen and uses batteries for mobile use. Small laptops are also called notebooks. The latest models can run as fast as similar desktop computers and have similar configurations. They are ideal for business executives who travel a lot.

A tablet PC is a type of notebook computer that has an LCD screen on which you can write with a stylus or digital pen. Your handwriting is recognized and converted into editable text. You can also input text by using speech recognition or a small keyboard. You can fold and rotate the screen easily.

Finally, a PDA is a lightweight, handheld computer. The letters stand for *personal digital assistant*. The term refers to a wide variety of handheld devices, including palmtops and pocket PCs. For input, you type using a small keyboard or you use a stylus – a special pen to select items on the screen. PDAs can be used as mobile phones, personal organizers or media players. They also let you access the Internet via Wi-Fi networks, and some include a GPS navigation system.

Inside the system

Topics
The CPU, the main memory, buses and cards
Units of memory
Your ideal computer system

Learning objectives
To understand the structure and functions of the CPU
To distinguish between RAM and ROM
To understand how memory is measured (bits, bytes, KB, MB, GB, TB)
To use relative pronouns correctly
To revise the basic components of a computer

Language
Grammar: Contextual reference
Defining relative clauses

Vocabulary: *processor, chip, control unit, arithmetic logic unit, register, expansion slot, motherboard, expansion card, system clock, bus, bus width, main memory, gigahertz*
Abbreviations and acronyms: *CPU, ALU, RAM, ROM, GHz, DIMM, BIOS, bit, KB, MB, GB, TB, ASCII*

Skills
Listening: Transferring information from a description to a diagram
Speaking: Describing one's ideal computer system
Reading: Understanding specific information
Writing: Making notes about one's ideal computer

Optional materials
A real processor chip, memory chips, ASCII code chart. Technical help is given on page 19.

Plan

Teacher's activities	Students' activities	Comments

1 Technical specifications
  A Elicit answers from SS. If you do not speak your SS' mother tongue, ask them to correct each other's work.
  B Monitor the task, helping with any vocabulary problems.
	A SS read the advertisement and translate the technical specs.
	B In pairs, SS try to answer the questions.
		A and **B** introduce words which appear in the reading passage; some may be new to SS. Refer SS to the Glossary if necessary.

2 What is inside a PC system?
  A Encourage SS to work out the meaning of unfamiliar words for themselves, but make it clear that they can ask questions if they need to.
  Ask SS to examine Figure 1, which illustrates the organization of a CPU.
  B Explain that reference markers (personal pronouns, demonstrative pronouns, etc.) provide discourse cohesion and help us understand the organization of ideas in a text.
	A Using the information in the text and Figure 1, SS answer the questions.
	B SS find out what the words in bold refer to.
		If you want to show SS the motherboard of a desktop PC, ask a computer science teacher to open a system unit so that SS can see the basic components. Remind them to take safety precautions (e.g. don't touch cables or switches).

3 Language work: defining relative clauses Refer SS to the HELP box, checking that they understand when the relative pronoun can be omitted (when it is the object of the clause).	SS complete the sentences with suitable relative pronouns.	Explain the difference between defining and non-defining relative clauses only if necessary.
4 How memory is measured **A** and **B** You may like to introduce the topic by writing the words *bits* and *bytes* on the board and asking SS to explain the difference. Monitor the tasks, helping with any vocabulary problems.	**A** SS read the text and answer the questions. **B** SS complete the sentences with the correct unit of memory.	Some SS may have problems with the concepts underlying this topic, as we are used to the decimal system not the binary system. Teach SS to count using binary digits if necessary. (see Technical help on page 19). Make sure SS understand the value of the different units of memory and how they are used to describe RAM, the size of a document, or the storage capacity of discs, MP3 players, etc.
5 A PC system **A** and **B** Monitor the tasks, helping where needed. Refer SS back to previous units for help if necessary. You may like to draw the diagram on the board. **C** Play track 4 of the CD for SS to check their answers.	**A** SS complete the diagram. **B** SS compare answers in pairs. **C** SS listen and check their answers.	This task revises the constituent parts of a computer system.
6 Your ideal computer system **A** Monitor the task, helping with any vocabulary problems. **B** Refer SS to the *Useful language* box. Monitor the discussions, checking SS are using the vocabulary correctly.	**A** SS make notes about their ideal computer. **B** SS then describe it to their partners.	

Evaluation of the unit:

Answer key

1 Technical specifications

A

Open task

B

1 The main function of a computer's processor is to process the instructions provided by the software; it also coordinates the activities of the other units.
2 The gigahertz (GHz). 1GHz is equivalent to 1000MHz.
3 RAM stands for *random access memory*.

2 What is inside a PC system?

A

1 The control unit, the ALU and the registers
2 Arithmetic logic unit; it performs mathematical calculations and logical operations
3 To measure and synchronize the flow of data
4 One thousand million hertz, or cycles, per second
5 RAM (random access memory)
6 ROM (read only memory)
7 By adding extra chips, usually contained in a small circuit board called a DIMM
8 Motherboard
9 An electrical path or channel that allows devices to communicate with each other
10 They allow you to install expansion cards (for example, sound, memory or network cards)

B

1 the CPU, or central processing unit
2 a single chip
3 the instruction
4 the computer's
5 a program
6 devices (inside the computer)

3 Language work: defining relative clauses

1 (which/that)
2 which/that
3 who/that
4 which/that
5 (which/that)
6 who/that

4 How memory is measured

A

1 A binary system uses two digits: 0 and 1. Switches inside a computer can only be in one of two possible states: OFF or ON. To represent these two conditions, we use binary notation. 0 means OFF and 1 means ON.
2 Each 0 or 1 is called a binary digit, or bit.
3 A byte
4 American Standard Code for Information Interchange
5 To provide a standard system for the representation of characters

B

1 terabyte
2 megabyte
3 kilobyte
4 gigabyte
5 byte

5 A PC system

A

1 Software
2 Hardware
3 CPU
4 Peripherals
5 RAM
6 Input devices
7 Storage devices
8 Mouse
9 Monitor
10 Hard drive

B

Open task

C

SS listen and check their answers to A.

6 Your ideal computer system

A and B

Open tasks

Audio script

… as you can see on the diagram, a PC system consists of two parts: software and hardware. Software is the programs that enable a computer to perform a specific task; this includes the operating system, and application software such as a graphics package and a web browser.

Hardware is any electronic or mechanical part. The basic structure of a computer system is made up of three main hardware sections: one, the central processing unit – or CPU – two, the main memory, and three, the peripherals.

The CPU is a processor chip which executes program instructions and coordinates the activities of all the other components. In order to improve the computer's performance, the user can add expansion cards for video, sound and networking.

The main memory holds the instructions and the data which are currently being processed by the CPU. This internal memory is made up of ROM and RAM chips. RAM, or random access memory, is volatile, so it loses the stored data when the electricity – or power – is turned off. ROM, or read-only memory, is non-volatile.

The peripherals are the physical units attached to the computer. They include input, output and storage devices. Input devices, for example the keyboard and the mouse, enable us to present information to the computer. Output devices allow us to extract the results from the computer. For instance, we can see the output on the monitor or in printed form. Storage devices are used to store information permanently. For example, we use hard disks, DVDs or flash drives to store large amounts of information.

Photocopiable © Cambridge University Press 2008

Technical help: Binary code

A computer can only manipulate 1s and 0s in order to process information. A 1 is represented by current flowing through a wire and a 0 by no current flowing through the wire. Sometimes 1 is referred to as a high voltage and 0 is referred as a low voltage. Everything about computers is based upon this binary process.

Each digit – 1 or 0 – is called a **bit**. Eight bits together are called a **byte**. The ASCII code is just a standard system to represent characters as bytes of binary signals.

ASCII, which stands for American Standard Code for Information Interchange, permits computers from different manufacturers to exchange data. ASCII uses 7-digit binary numbers to represent the letters of the alphabet, the numbers 0 to 9, various punctuation marks and symbols, and some special functions, such as the carriage return. Seven digits in binary implies that ASCII has room for 128 characters or symbols (with seven places to arrange 1s and 0s, we can make 128 possible code combinations). The eighth, or left-most bit of each byte, is often used to make sure the other seven bits are sent and received correctly (see the illustration to the right). Some programs use this bit for specific purposes.

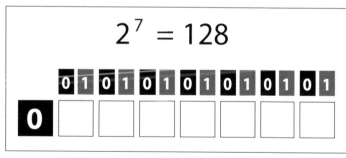

$$2^7 = 128$$

When you press a key on the computer keyboard, your program translates that key press into an ASCII code. This code can represent a character or a function to be performed (see the illustration to the right).

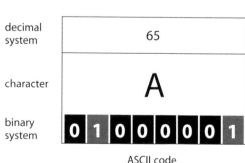

decimal system	65
character	A
binary system	0 1 0 0 0 0 0 1

ASCII code

Photocopiable © Cambridge University Press 2008

ASCII code chart

b7		0	0	0	0	1	1	1	1
	b6	0	0	1	1	0	0	1	1
	b5	0	1	0	1	0	1	0	1
BITS		Control		Symbols		UPPER CASE		Lower case	
b4 b3 b2 b1		special characters		Numbers		characters		characters	
0 0 0 0		NUL $_0$	DLE $_{16}$	SP $_{32}$	0 $_{48}$	@ $_{64}$	P $_{80}$	' $_{96}$	p $_{112}$
0 0 0 1		SOH $_1$	DC1 $_{17}$	! $_{33}$	1 $_{49}$	A $_{65}$	Q $_{81}$	a $_{97}$	q $_{113}$
0 0 1 0		STX $_2$	DC2 $_{18}$	" $_{34}$	2 $_{50}$	B $_{66}$	R $_{82}$	b $_{98}$	r $_{114}$
0 0 1 1		ETX $_3$	DC3 $_{19}$	# $_{35}$	3 $_{51}$	C $_{67}$	S $_{83}$	c $_{99}$	s $_{115}$
0 1 0 0		EOT $_4$	DC4 $_{20}$	$ $_{36}$	4 $_{52}$	D $_{68}$	T $_{84}$	d $_{100}$	t $_{116}$
0 1 0 1		ENQ $_5$	NAK $_{21}$	% $_{37}$	5 $_{53}$	E $_{69}$	U $_{85}$	e $_{101}$	u $_{117}$
0 1 1 0		ACK $_6$	SYN $_{22}$	& $_{38}$	6 $_{54}$	F $_{70}$	V $_{86}$	f $_{102}$	v $_{118}$
0 1 1 1		BEL $_7$	ETB $_{23}$	' $_{39}$	7 $_{55}$	G $_{71}$	W $_{87}$	g $_{103}$	w $_{119}$
1 0 0 0		BS $_8$	CAN $_{24}$	($_{40}$	8 $_{56}$	H $_{72}$	X $_{88}$	h $_{104}$	x $_{120}$
1 0 0 1		HT $_9$	EM $_{25}$	) $_{41}$	9 $_{57}$	I $_{73}$	Y $_{89}$	i $_{105}$	y $_{121}$
1 0 1 0		LF $_{10}$	SUB $_{26}$	* $_{42}$	: $_{58}$	J $_{74}$	Z $_{90}$	j $_{106}$	z $_{122}$
1 0 1 1		VT $_{11}$	ESC $_{27}$	+ $_{43}$	; $_{59}$	K $_{75}$	[$_{91}$	k $_{107}$	{ $_{123}$
1 1 0 0		FF $_{12}$	FS $_{28}$	, $_{44}$	< $_{60}$	L $_{76}$	\ $_{92}$	l $_{108}$	| $_{124}$
1 1 0 1		CR $_{13}$	GS $_{29}$	- $_{45}$	= $_{61}$	M $_{77}$	] $_{93}$	m $_{109}$	} $_{125}$
1 1 1 0		SO $_{14}$	RS $_{30}$	. $_{46}$	> $_{62}$	N $_{78}$	^ $_{94}$	n $_{110}$	~ $_{126}$
1 1 1 1		SI $_{15}$	US $_{31}$	/ $_{47}$	? $_{63}$	O $_{79}$	- $_{95}$	o $_{111}$	DEL $_{127}$

Key

binary

binary	**character** decimal

Notations

ASCII codes are conventionally expressed in decimal notation because decimal numbers are more convenient for people to recognize and interpret than binary numbers (see the ASCII code chart on page 20).

In programming, it is also common to represent binary codes by means of hexadecimal or octal notations. In hexadecimal notation, 16 is the base, or radix. The ten digits 0 to 9 are used, and in addition six more digits, usually A, B, C, D, E and F, to represent 10, 11, 12, 13, 14 and 15 as single characters. Octal notation uses eight digits: 0, 1, 2, 3, 4, 5, 6, 7.

These notations are used to write software, as a shorthand way of representing long strings of bits. Thus the string 01000001 can be represented as octal 101, decimal 65 and hexadecimal 41.

Binary	Octal	Decimal	Hexadecimal
0000000	000	000	00
0000001	001	001	01
0000010	002	002	02
0000011	003	003	03
0000100	004	004	04
0000101	005	005	05
0000110	006	006	06
0000111	007	007	07
0001000	010	008	08
0001001	011	009	09
0001010	012	010	0A
0001011	013	011	0B
0001100	014	012	0C
0001101	015	013	0D
0001110	016	014	0E
0001111	017	015	0F
0010000	020	016	10

Octal and hexadecimal notations arose from the need to handle data in 8-bit and 16-bit microprocessors

Bits for pictures

Bits are also used to code pictures. The pixels displayed on the screen correspond to bits in the computer's video memory, held in the graphics adaptor or video card. The total number of colours which can be shown on the screen depends on this graphics adapter, which converts the bits into visual signals.

Each pixel is a certain combination of the three primary colours: red, green and blue. A graphics adapter with 1 bit per primary colour can generate up to 8, or 2^3 colours, as you can see from the table on the right. A graphics adapter with 8 bits per primary colour can generate 16.7 million or $(2^3)^8$ colours.

Colour	Red	Green	Blue
black	0	0	0
blue	0	0	1
green	0	1	0
cyan	0	1	1
red	1	0	0
magenta	1	0	1
yellow	1	1	0
white	1	1	1

One bit per primary colour

Buying a computer

Topics
> In a computer shop
> Computers for particular work situations

Learning objectives
> To learn how to enquire about computers in a shop
> To understand the technical specs of different computers
> To select the most suitable computers for particular people
> To revise basic vocabulary from Module 1

Language
> Language functions useful to a shop assistant (greeting and offering help, giving technical specs, describing, comparing)
> Language functions useful to a customer (explaining what you are looking for, asking for technical specs, asking about price)

Skills
> **Listening:** Listening for specific information and language in a dialogue
> Taking notes about users' computer needs
> **Speaking:** Role play in a computer shop
> **Reading:** Understanding technical specifications
> **Writing:** Writing an email to a friend recommending a computer

Plan

Teacher's activities	Students' activities	Comments
1 In a computer shop **A** and **B** Elicit answers from SS and write relevant ideas on the board. **C** Play track 5 of the CD and ask SS the question: *Do they buy anything?* **D** Play the CD again, pausing if necessary. **E** Play the CD a third time. You may like to ask two SS to read the extract aloud to check answers.	**A** SS work individually as they list items that would improve their digital life. They then compare their choices in pairs. **B** SS think of three basic features or components that would make a big difference when buying a computer. **C** SS listen and answer the question. **D** SS listen again and complete the product descriptions. **E** SS listen to part of the dialogue and complete it.	As an introduction, you may like to ask SS this question: *Do you usually buy ICT devices in a computer shop or over the Internet?* Help SS distinguish between real information and expressions used to maintain a conversation, e.g. *um, well, I mean.*
2 Language functions in a computer shop Refer SS to the HELP box and read through the language functions. Point out that there is only one mistake in each sentence.	SS correct the mistakes in the sentences and then decide which functions are being expressed in each sentence.	Tasks 2 and 3 will help SS acquire the language they need in order to buy a computer. The appropriate use of these language functions will help SS develop their linguistic and strategic competence in communication. If students are having difficulties spotting the mistakes in Task 2, point out that they can find all of the answers by reading the HELP box carefully.

3 Role play – buying a computer Give SS time to read the information and instructions. Monitor the task, checking pronunciation and the correct use of lexis and structures from the HELP box.	In pairs, SS do the role play, following the instructions.	With more able SS, you may want to leave the task open – without the guided steps – so that SS can be as creative as they want.
4 Choosing the right computer **A** Play track 6 of the CD. Ask SS to justify their choices. **B** Refer SS back to their work in Unit 3, Task 6. Monitor the discussions, helping where needed.	**A** SS first listen to four people talking about their computer needs and take notes. They then read the descriptions of four computers on a website and, in pairs, choose the most suitable computer for each person. **B** SS choose the computer closest to the ideal system they described in Unit 3.	Many people now buy things over the Internet instead of going to a shop. E-commerce is studied in Unit 17.
5 Vocabulary tree You may like to ask a student to draw the tree on the board. Encourage SS to construct similar trees for other topics in the course.	SS insert the words in the appropriate place on the vocabulary tree.	Tasks 5 and 6 allow you to check that SS have understood the concepts and information introduced in this module.
6 Recommending a computer You may like to set this task for homework. **Online task** Visit www.cambridge.org/elt/ict for an online task related to the topic of this module.	SS write an email recommending a computer to a friend.	

Evaluation of the unit:

Answer key

1 In a computer shop

A

Possible answers

A portable hard drive, a new printer, a digital camera, an MP3 player, etc.

B

Possible answers

The type of processor and its speed; the amount of RAM; the hard drive capacity; internet capabilities (for example, Wi-Fi)

C

No, they don't buy anything

D

iMac

Processor speed **2.33GHz**
RAM **2GB**
Hard drive capacity **500GB**
DVD drive included? **Yes**
Operating system **Mac OS**
Includes internet software
Price **£819**

MacBook

Processor speed **2.0GHz**
RAM **1GB**
Hard drive capacity **160GB**
DVD drive included? **Yes**
Operating system **Mac OS**
Includes internet software
Price **£1,029**

E

1 help
2 models
3 operating
4 running
5 fast
6 expanded
7 suitable
8 practical

2 Language functions in a computer shop

1 The Ulysses SD is a **powerful**, expandable computer that offers high-end graphics at a low price. (**Describing**)
2 A laptop is likely to be more expensive than the equivalent desktop, but a laptop is **more** practical if you travel a lot. (**Comparing**)
3 **What's** the storage capacity of the hard drive? (**Asking for technical specs**)
4 I'm looking **for** a desktop PC that has good graphics for games. (**Explaining what you are looking for**)
5 Do you need **any** help? (**Greeting and offering help**)
6 And how **much** does the PDA cost? (**Asking the price**)
7 The workstation **has** a Pentium processor with dual-core technology, 1,024 gigabytes of RAM, and 1 terabyte of disk space. (**Giving technical specs**)

3 Role play – buying a computer

Open task

4 Choosing the right computer

A

Speaker 1: Gateway C-120 convertible notebook
Speaker 2: Dell Inspiron 531 desktop PC
Speaker 3: Sun workstation
Speaker 4: Sony Vaio AR laptop

B

Open task

5 Vocabulary tree

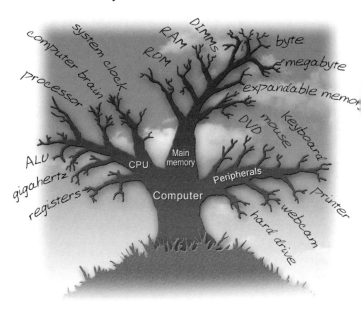

6 Recommending a computer

Open task

Audio script

Task 1

Assistant: Do you need any help?

Paul: Um, yes, we're looking for a Mac computer. Have you got any fairly basic ones?

Assistant: Yes, sure. If you'd like to come over here …

Paul: What different models are there?

Assistant: At the moment we've got these two models: the iMac, which is a desktop computer with an Intel Core 2 Duo processor operating at 2.33 gigahertz, and the portable MacBook, which has a processor running at 2.0 gigahertz. Core Duo technology actually means two cores, or processors, built into a single chip, offering up to twice the speed of a traditional chip.

Sue: So they're both very fast, then. And which one has more memory? I mean, which has more RAM?

Assistant: Well, the iMac has two gigabytes of RAM, which can be expanded up to three gigabytes, and the MacBook has one gigabyte, expandable to two gigabytes. It all depends on your needs. The iMac is suitable for home users and small offices. The MacBook is more practical if you travel a lot.

Sue: And what's the storage capacity of the hard drive?

Assistant: The iMac has a storage capacity of 500 gigabytes, and the MacBook has a hard drive of 160 gigabytes.

Sue: Do they have a DVD drive?

Assistant: Yes, they each come with a DVD SuperDrive that lets you burn all types of DVDs and CDs. And they feature a camera built right into the display so you can start a video chat instantly.

Sue: And how much do they cost?

Assistant: The iMac is £819 and the MacBook is £1,029. They both come with wireless networking and Bluetooth.

Paul: What about the operating system?

Assistant: Well, every Mac comes with the latest version of Mac OS pre-installed; that includes internet software and some programs to organize and edit your photos, music and movies.

Paul: OK, well, thanks very much. I think we need to go away and think about it for a bit.

Audio script

Task 4

1

I'm still at university and I need an ultra-light computer that I can easily take to class. I need to write essays and web-based projects, and I'd also like to be able to take notes and draw directly on the screen. What would you recommend …

2

I manage an advertising company so I need a powerful system that'll work with multimedia applications, integrating text and pictures with animation and voice annotations. Digitized images and sound occupy a lot of disk space so I imagine I'll have to have a lot of…

3

I work as a CAD engineer and my job involves computer-aided design, simulations, geoscience and engineering. Those applications obviously require a lot of memory and a large drive so I need something …

4

I'm a sales representative for a paper company, and I'm always travelling. I'm looking for a lightweight machine which I can use to process orders and communicate with head office while I'm on the road. Is there anything you can recommend? My budget …

2 Input/Output devices

Learning objectives

In this module, you will:

- describe input and output devices.
- identify the different keys on a keyboard and explain their functions.
- distinguish between facts and opinions in advertisements.
- learn how to understand the technical specs of digital cameras, printers and display devices.
- learn and use the superlative form of adjectives.
- practise recommending the most suitable display device for particular people.
- learn how to understand and give instructions and advice for the use of computers and monitors.
- compare different types of printer.
- learn and use discourse connectors.
- learn about what sort of input/output devices disabled people can use.

Type, click and talk!

Topics
Input devices: the keyboard, the mouse, etc.
Voice input

Learning objectives
To be able to describe input devices
To identify different keys on a keyboard
To understand basic mouse actions
To understand the use of speech recognition systems

Language
Grammar: Describing function: *for + -ing;* relative pronoun + verb; relative pronoun + *is used + to +* infinitive; *used + to +* infinitive
Describing features: *It has … It features … It allows you to …*
Vocabulary: *keyboard, mouse, scanner, trackball, graphics tablet, light pen, joystick, game controller, barcode reader, touchpad, touch screen, webcam, microphone*
Groups of keys: *alphanumeric, function,* etc.
Mouse actions: *select, click, double-click, drag,* etc.

Skills
Listening: Identifying particular devices from their descriptions
Identifying what is and isn't mentioned in an interview
Speaking: Describing input devices
Reading: Identifying keys on a diagram from information in a text
Reading and filling in the gaps in a text
Writing: Describing a game controller

Optional materials
Real input devices (mouse, microphone, etc.)
A standard keyboard

Plan

Teacher's activities	Students' activities	Comments
Module page You may want to point out the learning objectives to your SS.	SS familiarize themselves with the topics and objectives of the Module.	
1 Interacting with your computer Introduce the topic by directing SS' attention to the pictures. Then ask SS to read the introductory definition. Explain *input* in contrast to *output* by using examples (keyboard = input; monitor = output)	SS look at the illustrations and try to name the devices.	The introduction does not include all input devices. Other devices include: *touchpad, touch screen, webcam* and *barcode reader.* These are presented in Task 3B.
2 Describing input devices **A** Play track 7 of the CD, pausing after each description. **B** Play the CD again.	**A** SS listen and identify the three input devices. **B** SS listen again and complete the extracts.	

3 Describing functions and features

A Refer SS to the HELP box or write the syntactic patterns on the board. Check that SS understand the use of *to +* infinitive (see *Comments*).

B Monitor the task, checking that SS are using suitable structures for describing the objects.

A SS use the notes to write a description of the Sony Playstation 3 controller.

B SS work in pairs. One person describes the function and features of a device, the other person guesses what it is.

B is designed to help SS describe computer devices. Some students will produce incorrect sentences like *for to control*.

4 The keyboard

A If possible, show SS a real keyboard. Ask them to check if the illustration in their books is an exact reproduction of the real thing.

B Encourage SS to record these new terms in their vocabulary books and to learn them. Make sure SS can match the keys (a–h) with the actual keys in the illustration on page 24.

A SS label the picture of a standard keyboard with the groups of keys.

B SS match the descriptions with the names of the keys and then find the keys in the illustration of the keyboard in 4a.

Some SS may want to talk about the purpose of some *dedicated* keys, such as *Ctrl, Alt, Alt gr*. Encourage them to explain the function of these keys in their own words, using language from Task 3.

The layout of a keyboard can vary from country to country.

The cursor control keys are the arrow keys (↑, ↓, ←, →), *Pg Up, Pg Down, Home, End, Ins* and *Del*.
The layout of alphanumeric keys is known as QWERTY because the first six letters at the top left of the keyboard are the letters *Q, W, E, R, T* and *Y*.
The function keys are *F1–F12*.
The dedicated keys are *Ctrl, Alt, Alt Gr, Esc, Enter (Return), Tab, Caps Lock, Shift, Print Screen* and *Scroll Lock*.

5 Mouse actions

Monitor the task, helping with any vocabulary problems.

SS read the text and fill in the gaps with verbs from the box.

If you have access to computers in class, practise SS' understanding of the terms by giving them instructions to carry out using the mouse, for example: *Double-click the hard drive icon*.

Make sure SS understand the basic mouse techniques: *select, click, double-click, drag* and *grab*.

6 Speech recognition systems

A Ask SS if they have ever used their voice to input data. Go through the list of features before playing track 8 of the CD.

B Read the questions before playing the CD again.

C Monitor the discussions, helping where needed.

A SS listen and tick the features mentioned in the interview.

B SS listen again and answer the questions.

C In groups, SS discuss the questions.

Some SS may find this task difficult. In this case, give them a copy of the audio script to read while they are listening.

Evaluation of the unit:

Answer key

1 Interacting with your computer

1 light pen
2 game controller
3 scanner
4 mouse
5 keyboard
6 graphics tablet
7 trackball
8 microphone

2 Describing input devices

A

1 keyboard
2 mouse
3 light pen

B

1 used to
2 have; for
3 for controlling
4 features
5 can
6 works by
7 allows; to

3 Describing functions and features

A

Possible answer

The PlayStation 3 controller is an input device used to control video games on the Sony PlayStation 3. It is held with both hands and the thumbs are used to handle the direction and action buttons. It has a six-axis sensing system, which allows the user to move the controller in six different directions: up, down, left, right, forwards and backwards.

The PS3 controller operates wirelessly via Bluetooth, but it features a USB mini port and USB cable which can be connected to the PlayStation for wired play and for charging the internal battery.

B

Open task

4 About the keyboard

A

a 2　　b 3　　c 5　　d 1　　e 4

B

1f　　2b　　3h　　4g　　5d　　6c　　7e　　8a

5 Mouse actions

1 control
2 move
3 click
4 select
5 drag
6 grab
7 double-click

6 Speech recognition systems

A

Speech recognition systems:

✔ need a good sound card and a microphone.
✔ can take dictation with accuracy.
✘ allow you to create and compile a computer program.
✔ allow you to execute programs and navigate around menus using voice commands.
✔ allow you to surf the Web by speaking.
✘ allow you to design graphics.

B

1 The keyboard and the mouse
2 By using a high-quality headset microphone
3 Around 98%
4 By reading aloud sample text for a few minutes
5 Proper names, abbreviations and unusual words

C

Open task

Audio script

Task 2

1

This device is used to enter information into the computer. As well as having normal typewriter keys for characters and a numeric keypad, it may also have function keys and editing keys for special purposes.

2

This is a device for controlling the cursor and selecting items on the screen. The ball underneath is rolled in any direction across the surface of a desk to move the cursor on the screen. It may have an optical sensor instead of a ball. It usually features two buttons and a wheel. By clicking a button, the user can activate icons or select items and text. A wireless version works without cables.

3

In shape, this input device is similar to an ordinary pen. It works by detecting light from the computer screen and is used by pointing it directly at the screen display. It allows the user to answer multiple-choice questions and to draw diagrams or graphics.

Audio script

Task 6

Interviewer: Now, mobile phones and the Internet have changed the way we all communicate. However, we still need to use a keyboard and a mouse to communicate with computers. When will we be able to interact with PCs by voice?

Anne: Well, the technology already exists, but the habit of talking to a computer is only just beginning to take off.

Interviewer: What are the basic components of a speech recognition system?

Anne: Basically, you need voice recognition software, a sound card and a microphone. If you want to have good results, you should get a high quality headset microphone.

Interviewer: Right. What sort of things can you do with a speech recognition system?

Anne: The system converts voice into text, so you can dictate text directly onto your word processor or email program. The technology is particularly useful for dictating notes, business memos, letters and email.

Interviewer: But is dictation accurate? I mean, does the system interpret all the words correctly?

Anne: Speech companies claim an accuracy rate of around 98 per cent. But the system is more accurate if you train the software by reading aloud sample text for a few minutes. This process teaches the program to recognize words that are not in its built-in dictionary, for example proper names, abbreviations, unusual words, etc.

Interviewer: I see. And can you execute programs and navigate around menus and windows?

Anne: Yes, you can control your PC by voice commands. This means you can launch programs, open a file, save it in a particular format or print it. Some systems even let you search the Web by voice or chat using your voice instead of the keyboard.

Interviewer: That does sound exciting.

Unit 6 — Capture your favourite image

Topics
Scanners, digital cameras, video cameras

Learning objectives
To understand spoken and written texts about scanners and digital cameras
To distinguish between facts and opinions in adverts
To describe a digital camera
To use the superlative form of adjectives correctly
To use suffixes correctly

Language
Grammar: The superlative form of adjectives

Vocabulary:
scan, flatbed scanner, slide scanner, handheld scanner, OCR, digitized image, digital camera, camcorder (video camera), camera phone, megapixel
Suffixes to form adjectives and nouns.
Persuasive language in adverts

Skills
Listening: Completing notes based on a conversation
Speaking: Describing features of a digital camera
Reading: Finding specific information in a text
Distinguishing facts and opinions in adverts
Writing: Completing a press release

Optional materials
Adverts from specialist computer magazines

Plan

Teacher's activities	Students' activities	Comments
1 The eyes of your computer **A** Elicit answers from SS and write them on the board. You may like to also ask SS the question: *Why are scanners and cameras called the 'eyes of your computer'?* **B** Encourage SS to read the text quickly. They will be reading it in more detail in Task C. **C** Monitor the task, helping with any vocabulary problems.	**A** In pairs, SS discuss different ways of capturing an image on a computer. **B** SS read the text and see how many things from their list in A are mentioned. **C** Using the information in the texts and the illustrations, SS answer the questions.	You may like to explain the word *scanner*. The verb *scan* has two different meanings: when you *scan* written material, you look through it in order to find important information; if a machine *scans* something, it reads or examines it very quickly, by moving a beam of light over it.
2 Scanners Ask SS to read the notes before listening. Play track 9 of CD, pausing if necessary.	SS listen to the conversation and complete the notes.	You may like to give SS a copy of the audio script.
3 Facts and opinions **A** Elicit answers from SS. Make the difference between facts and opinions clear. **B** You may like to draw a table on the board and write the facts and opinions in different columns. **C** Ask SS to justify their answers.	**A** SS complete the definitions. **B** SS read the adverts, underline the facts and circle the opinions. **C** SS compare their answers and decide which text is more factual or objective, and which one uses more persuasive language.	This task aims to point out the difference between facts and opinions and to highlight the persuasive language used in advertisements.

4 Language work: superlatives **A** and **B** 　Encourage SS to explain the rules themselves before referring them to the HELP box. **C** Monitor the discussions, checking that SS are using the superlative forms correctly.	**A** SS read the examples and deduce the grammatical rules for forming superlatives. **B** SS complete the sentences with the superlative form of the adjectives in brackets. **C** In pairs, SS discuss the situations using the superlative.	If SS are struggling with Task A, encourage them to use their mother tongue. The comparative form is studied in Unit 8.
5 Language work: suffixes **A** Refer SS to the HELP box, providing more examples if necessary. **B** Encourage SS to use dictionaries if necessary.	**A** SS use suitable suffixes to make adjectives or nouns. **B** SS complete the sentences with the word in brackets and a suffix from the list.	Remind SS of the importance of word formation processes in helping them to build a larger vocabulary and recognize new, unknown words.
6 Press release: a digital camera Monitor the task, helping with any vocabulary problems.	SS choose words from the box and complete the description.	
7 Describing a camera Monitor the activity, helping where needed. You may like to ask SS to bring in their own cameras to describe.	In pairs, SS describe a digital camera, webcam or video camera.	SS may need help with the technical specs of cameras: *megapixels, optical zoom, flash memory cards,* etc. Refer SS to the Glossary if necessary.

Evaluation of the unit:

Answer key

1 The eyes of your computer

A

Possible answers

A scanner, a digital camera, a webcam, a camera phone, a bar code reader

B

SS read the text and check their answers to A.

C

1 A scanner

2 The scanner reads the image or text, converts it into a series of dots and then generates a digitized image which is sent to the computer and stored.
3 Digital cameras don't use film. Photos are stored in the camera's memory card as digital data (binary codes).
4 A built-in camera
5 A camcorder, or digital video camera
6 Video editing software

2 Scanners

1 photocopier
2 computer
3 OCR (optical character recognition)
4 text, colour pictures and even small 3-D objects
5 35mm slides
6 small pictures or logos

3 Facts and opinions

A

1 facts
2 opinions

B

ColourScan XR
Facts:

… a flatbed scanner
1,200 dpi of resolution
9"x15" of scanning area
You can enter data and graphic images directly into your applications
… comes complete with its own image capture software, which allows for colour and grey retouching

Opinions:

You can get crisp, clean scans …
… it's easy to use.
It couldn't be cheaper.
… the ColourScan XR is the clear winner.

ScanPress DF
Facts:

… a self-calibrating flatbed scanner
2,400 dpi of resolution
You can scan everything from black and white to 24-bit colour
Comes with a hardware accelerator for JPEG compression and decompression
JPEG technology saves disk space by compressing images by up to 50 to 1.
… comes with OCR software and Photoshop.

Opinions:

… we have chosen the most advanced technology …
… the best scans with the least effort.
It produces images with high colour definition and sharpness.
… a fantastic machine that you will love working with.
… an excellent investment.

C
Open task

4 Language work: superlatives

A
SS read the HELP box to check their answers.

B

1 fastest; highest
2 most revolutionary
3 easiest
4 best; the least
5 most modern

C

Open task

5 Language work: suffixes

A

1 colourful (adj); coloured (adj)
2 professional (adj)
3 photographic (adj); photographer (noun)
4 wired (adj); wireless (adj)
5 blurry (adj); blurred (adj)
6 innovative (adj); innovation (noun); innovator (noun)
7 underexposure (noun); underexposed (adj)

B

1 manufacturer
2 reduction
3 Cropping
4 sharpness
5 technology

6 Press release: a digital camera

1 megapixels
2 optical
3 brighter
4 colour
5 shot
6 reduction
7 video

7 Describing a camera

Open task

Audio script

Student: What sort of technology is used in scanners?

Vicky: Well, a scanner is a bit like a photocopier. You put the image you want to copy face down on the glass plate of the scanner, start the program, and a laser beam reads the image in horizontal lines. This image is then sent to the computer where you can see it, and then manipulate it as you want.

Student: What about text? Can you scan text?

Vicky: Yes, you can, but you need special software called OCR – optical character recognition. This interprets the text letter by letter and enables the computer to recognize the characters.

Student: Why do people need to scan text?

Vicky: Well, text that's been scanned can be stored as data in databases, or edited with a word processor.

Student: Um, OK. What types of scanner are there?

Vicky: Well, there are three basic types: flatbed scanners, slide scanners and handheld scanners. Flatbed scanners are built like a photocopier and are for use on a desktop. They can scan text, colour pictures and even small three-dimensional objects. They're very convenient and versatile. Slide scanners are used to scan 35mm slides or film negatives. They work at very high resolution, so they're more expensive than flatbeds. Handheld scanners are small, compact and T-shaped. The scanning head isn't as wide as the one in a flatbed – they can only copy images up to about four inches wide. They're used for capturing small pictures and logos.

Display screens and ergonomics

Topics
How screen displays work
Health and safety with computers

Learning objectives
To understand how a computer display works
To recommend the most suitable display for particular people
To write a list of guides to make your school or office more ergonomic
To understand instructions and advice for the use of computers and monitors

Language
Grammar: Instructions and advice: imperatives, *should, ought to, had better*
Vocabulary: *pixel, resolution, flicker, phosphor, electron beam, ergonomics, tilt-and-swivel, aspect ratio, colour depth, video adapter, plasma screen, inch, video projector, home cinema*
Abbreviations: *CRT, LCD, TFT, OLED, cd/m2, RSI*

Skills
Listening: Listening for specific information in order to complete sentences
Speaking: Describing a computer screen
Discussing which display devices one would like to own
Reading: Understanding specific information and technical specs
Writing: Writing a description from information in a table
Writing a list of recommendations for an ergonomic school or office

Optional materials
Technical specs of an LCD monitor
Printed web pages about health and safety with computers or ergonomics

Plan

Teacher's activities	Students' activities	Comments
1 Your computer screen Elicit answers from SS.	SS use the questions to describe their computer screen to another student.	The size of a monitor is measured in inches (") diagonally across the screen (15", 17", etc.). One inch equals 2.54 cm.
2 How screen displays work **A** Encourage SS to read the text quickly to check their answers. They will be reading it in more detail in Task B. **B** Remind SS to use the context to guess unfamiliar words. It is possible to do the task without understanding every word. Check answers with the whole class.	**A** SS complete the definitions with words from the box. SS then read the text to check their answers. **B** SS read the text again and answer the questions.	This is quite a technical topic. Help SS to understand basic terms like *resolution, pixel, aspect ratio, screen size* and *colour depth* by referring them to the Glossary if necessary.

3 Choosing the right display device **A** Play track 10 of the CD. Next, read the descriptions of the five display devices and play the CD again. Ask SS to justify their choices. **B** Monitor the discussions, asking SS to justify their choices.	**A** SS listen to five users describing their display device needs. SS then read the descriptions of five devices and choose the most suitable device for each person. **B** In pairs, SS choose the system they would most like to own, explaining why.	You may like to discuss the benefits of interactive whiteboards in education. You may also like to ask SS the question: *Describe the home cinema system of your dreams.*
4 Ergonomics **A** You may like to personalize the task by asking questions like: *Do you use computers a lot? Have you had any problems from using PCs or mobile phones?* Play track 11 of the CD and ask SS the question: *What health problems do they mention?* **B** Play the CD again, pausing if necessary. **C** Draw SS' attention to the illustration and play the CD again.	**A** SS look at the illustration and talk about their own experience. SS then listen to the conversation and answer the question. **B** SS listen again and complete the extracts. **C** SS match the extracts from B with the correct part of the diagram.	You may like to give SS a copy of the audio script.
5 Language work: instructions and advice **A** Refer SS to the HELP box, checking that they understand the use of the imperative, *should/shouldn't* and *it's a good/ bad idea to …* **B** Monitor the task, checking that SS are using the language from the HELP box correctly.	**A** SS complete some health and safety guidelines using *should/ shouldn't.* **B** In pairs, SS practise giving advice about how to use a monitor safely.	This task revises the grammatical forms used to give instructions and advice. The task is directly related to the listening passage.
6 An ergonomic school or office Monitor the task, helping where needed. You may like to set this task for homework.	SS write an email to their teacher/ manager including a list of guidelines for making their school or office more ergonomic.	You may like to ask SS to make a poster with health and safety tips for their office or an ICT classroom at their school/college.

Evaluation of the unit:

Answer key

1 Your computer screen

Open task

2 How screen displays work

A

1 pixel
2 video adapter
3 aspect ration
4 plasma screen
5 resolution
6 colour depth

B

1 CRT stands for Cathode Ray Tube; LCD stands for Liquid Crystal Display.
2 The screen size is measured diagonally (in inches).
3 Active-matrix LCDs use TFT (thin film transistor) technology, in which each pixel has its own switch.
4 Brightness, or luminance, is measured in cd/m2 (candela per square metre).
5 Phosphor
6 They consume less power, produce brighter colours and are flexible, so they can be bent when not in use.

3 Choosing the right display device

A

Speaker 1: d
Speaker 2: b
Speaker 3: e
Speaker 4: a
Speaker 5: c

B

Open task

4 Ergonomics

A

Sore, tired eyes; repetitive strain injury (RSI); occasional headaches

B

1 supports; adjustable
2 on the floor
3 at the same height as; parallel to
4 eye level
5 arm's length
6 up or around

C

a5   b4   c3   d6   e1   f2

5 Language work: instructions and advice

A

1 should
2 should
3 shouldn't
4 should
5 shouldn't

B

1 **You shouldn't / It's a bad idea to** open the monitor. It's dangerous.
2 **You shouldn't / It's a bad idea to** stare at the screen for long periods of time.
3 **You should / It's a good idea to** position the monitor at eye level or just below.
4 **You should / It's a good idea to** leave enough space behind the monitor for unobstructed movement.
5 **You shouldn't / It's a bad idea to** sit near the sides or back of CRT monitors. You should / It's a good idea to use LCD screens instead – they're free from radiation.
6 **You should / It's a good idea to** keep the screen clean to prevent distorting shadows.

6 An ergonomic school or office

Open task

Audio script

Task 3

1

I'm looking to create a home theatre system in my living room. I'd like a good set up for watching movies and sports in high-definition, listening to music, and playing games on my Xbox …

2

I need to do graphic design, including photo retouching, for a publishing company. I need a large monitor that can display two full-size pages side by side. I also like to watch DVDs on my computer so …

3

I prepare multimedia presentations with PowerPoint on my laptop, and I need to be able to display the images on a wall or screen …

4

I'd like to buy an entry-level monitor for everyday use. And I need one that doesn't take up a lot of space on my desk because it's only a very …

5

I teach Science, and I've been encouraged to use this new presentation tool. They say it can help me create really dynamic lessons …

Audio script

Task 4

Tony: There are a number of health and safety problems that may result from the continuous use of computers. Anyone spending more than four hours a day working on a PC may start to suffer from aching hands, neck or shoulders, occasional headaches, and eyestrain.

Worker one: Is there anything we can do to avoid it?

Tony: Yes, there's a lot you can do. For example, if you take the trouble to position your computer properly, you can avoid backache. Get a good chair, one that supports your lower back and is adjustable so you can change its height and angle. Make sure your feet rest firmly on the floor or on a footrest. Position the keyboard at the same height as your elbows, with your arms parallel to the work surface, and position the monitor at or just below eye level. You should look down at it slightly, not up. Don't put your monitor in front of a window, and make sure there isn't a lamp shining directly into your eyes or reflecting off the screen. You should sit at arm's length from the front of the monitor – about 50 to 70 centimetres away. It's a good idea to have a monitor with a tilt-and-swivel stand. Does anyone know what that is?

Worker two: Yes. I think it's a kind of stand that lets you move the monitor up or around, so you can use it at the correct angle and height.

Tony: That's right. Now, do you know of any health problems caused by using a computer?

Worker three: I've heard of something called RSI. But I'm not exactly sure what it is.

Tony: RSI stands for *repetitive strain injury*, and it causes pain in the upper arms and back. People who type constantly at high speed often suffer from it.

Worker four: My eyes often feel really sore and tired after I've been using the computer for a few hours. How do I stop that from happening?

Tony: Well, as a general rule, you shouldn't use a monitor that's fuzzy or that distorts the image. Give your eyes a rest. Look away from the monitor from time to time, out of the window or across the room.

Unit 8   Choosing a printer

Topics
Types of printer
Advertisements for printers

Learning objectives
To understand the most important technical features
   of printers
To compare different types of printer
To recognize and use discourse connectors
To use the comparative form of adjectives correctly

Language
  Grammar: Discourse cohesion: connectors
    Comparatives
  Vocabulary: Types of printer: *dot-matrix, inkjet, laser,*
    thermal, imagesetter, platesetter (CTP), multi-function
    printer, plotter
    Other terms: *output, resolution, scalable fonts,*
    dots per inch, ink cartridge, toner, PictBridge, page
    description language
    Abbreviations: *cps, dpi, USB, CTP, PDL*

Skills
  Listening: Understanding specific information from a
    podcast
  Speaking: Discussing which printer to choose for
    particular situations
    Describing your ideal printer
  Reading: Completing a table with technical
    information given in a text
    Scanning advertisements for information
    Analysing the function of linking words in a text
  Writing: Describing the printer(s) used at home
    or at work
    Writing an email to a friend comparing two printers

Optional materials
Advertisements taken from mass media or computer
   magazines

Plan

Teacher's activities	Students' activities	Comments

1 Types of printer
  A Elicit some types of printer and write them on the board.
  B You may need to pre-teach some of the key terms here: *inkjet, dot-matrix, pins*, etc.
  C Encourage SS to scan the text quickly for the words.
	A SS make a list of all the types of printer they can think of.
	  B SS label the illustrations.
	  C SS scan the text again and find words with the given meanings.
		The two most common types of printer are inkjets and laser printers.
		
		In publishing, the most recent technology is called *Computer to Plate*, or *CTP*, where images are created on a computer and output directly to the printing plates, without requiring film.

2 Language work: connectors 1
  A Refer SS to the HELP box, explaining that awareness of connectors can help them to develop their reading and writing skills.
  B Encourage SS to use dictionaries if necessary.
  C Encourage SS to use connectors to organize their writing. You may like to set this task for homework.
	A SS put the connectors into the correct columns.
	  B SS add some more connectors to each column and translate them into their own language.
	  C SS write a paragraph about the pros and cons of the printer(s) they use.
		There is more work on connectors in Unit 11.

3 Choosing the right printer
  A Ask SS to justify their choices. Accept different answers as long as they're justified.
  B Help SS with technical words by referring them to the Glossary if necessary. Encourage them to be as creative as they like.
	A SS choose the most suitable printer for particular situations.
	B SS describe their ideal printer to another student.	

4 Multi-function printers
  A Play track 12 of the CD and ask SS the question: *What two disadvantages are mentioned?*
  B Ask SS to read the questions before listening. Play the CD again, pausing if necessary.
	A SS listen to an extract from a podcast about multi-function printers and answer the question.
	B SS listen again and answer specific questions.
		Some SS may find this task a little difficult. Give them plenty of time to write their answers and supply the audio script if necessary.

5 Language work: comparatives Refer SS to the HELP box, providing more examples if necessary.	SS complete the sentences using the comparative form of the adjectives in brackets.	If SS are struggling, let them work in pairs.

6 Reading quiz – printer adverts
  A This is a competitive quiz, so you may like to set a reasonable time limit of, say, 6–7 minutes.
  B Monitor the task, helping SS where necessary. You may like to set this task for homework.
	A In pairs, SS go through the adverts until they find the specific information they are looking for.
	B SS write an email to a friend, comparing two printers and giving advice about which one to buy.
		These adverts are authentic, taken from the Web.

Evaluation of the unit:

Answer key

1 Types of printer

A

Open task

B

1 inkjet printer
2 laser printer
3 dot-matrix printer
4 plotter
5 imagesetter

Thermal transfer printers and platesetters aren't pictured.

C

1 graphics
2 resolution
3 hue
4 toner
5 scalable fonts
6 bar code
7 (printing) plate
8 intermediate

2 Language work: connectors 1

A

Giving examples	Listing/ Sequencing	Giving reason/ cause
such as	to begin with	since
for instance	then	because
for example	finally	*as*
including	*firstly, secondly, thirdly*, etc.	
	next	
	after that	
	at the end	

B

See words in italics in table above for possible answers

C

Open task

3 Choosing the right printer

A

Possible answers

1 An inkjet printer
2 A laser printer
3 A plotter
4 An imagesetter or platesetter

B

Open task

4 Multi-function printers

A

There are a lot of components in one machine, so if it breaks down, you may lose all of its functions at the same time; they can only do one thing at a time – for example, you can't print a document and receive a fax simultaneously.

B

1 A multi-function printer is an 'all-in-one' device that combines several functions into one unit – a printer, scanner, copier and fax.
2 Because they are cheap and versatile; all the components are well integrated.
3 PictBridge technology allows you to print directly from memory cards in cameras without connecting to a computer.
4 They can print envelopes, labels and even transparencies.
5 They usually come with a CD with the printer drivers, OCR, and photo and image software.
6 People spend a lot of money on ink cartridges so Mr Kelly recommends that users buy printers that use cheap cartridges.
7 An inkjet based model
8 A laser unit

5 Language work: comparatives

1 quieter
2 more expensive; greater
3 better; good
4 more reliable; easier
5 good
6 less accurate
7 heavier

6 Reading quiz – printer adverts

A

1 Two
2 The Vutek UltraVu II 5330
3 You can print on a wide variety of materials, including vinyl, pressure-sensitive paper, mesh and textiles.
4 PictBridge
5 PCL and PostScript
6 2,400 dpi
7 The network printer can print up to 31 ppm mono, 8 ppm colour (A4)

B

Open task

Audio script

Miranda: In the studio with me is John Kelly, from TextPrint. Mr Kelly, what exactly is a multi-function printer?

Mr Kelly: Well, essentially it's an 'all-in-one' device that can work as a scanner, a fax and a photocopier, as well as a printer.

Miranda: These devices are becoming very popular. What are the factors behind their success?

Mr Kelly: Basically, they're cheaper and more versatile than standalone products. The printing and scanning components are well integrated and they come with an LCD screen, slots for memory cards, and PictBridge connections.

Miranda: What's PictBridge, exactly?

Mr Kelly: It's a technology developed by Canon that lets you send images from a memory card in a digital camera or a camera phone directly to a printer. No computer is necessary. All you have to do is take pictures with your camera and connect it to a printer via a USB cable.

Miranda: And what kind of things can multi-function printers print? Can they just print sheets of paper or do they print other things as well?

Mr Kelly: Oh, yes, they can print envelopes, labels and even transparencies.

Miranda: Do multi-function printers have any downsides, or disadvantages?

Mr Kelly: Yes. There are a lot of components in one machine, so if it breaks down, you may lose all of its functions at the same time. Also, they can only do one thing at a time. For example, you can't print a document and receive a fax simultaneously.

Miranda: And what about software? Should I get any photo editing software if I buy a multi-function printer?

Mr Kelly: Well, they usually include a CD with the printer drivers, OCR, and photo and image software. You can do some basic editing, like adjusting brightness and removing red eyes. However, if you want better results, you'll need specialized software.

Miranda: What would your advice be to someone thinking about buying one of these devices?

Mr Kelly: Only a couple of things, really. Bear in mind that companies don't make money from the printer, but from the ink. If you print a lot, you'll spend a lot of money on cartridges. So consider buying printers with cheap ink cartridges. Finally, if you are a home user, you should go for an inkjet-based model. But for groupworks and businesses that need high-quality, low-cost-per-page output at large quantities, I'd recommend a laser unit.

Devices for the disabled

Topics
Assistive technology for disabled people
The Web Accessibility Initiative (WAI)

Learning objectives
To understand what sort of input/output devices disabled people can use
To talk and write about how computers can be adapted for blind, deaf and motor-impaired users

Language
Grammar: Noun phrases (range of modifiers: adjectives, participles, 's genitive, nouns)
Vocabulary: *Braille, embosser, speech synthesis system, screen magnifier, sip and puff, electronic note taker, textphone, on-screen keyboard, adaptive switch, eyegaze system, touch screen, voice recognition system*

Skills
Listening: Listening to an interview and taking notes
Speaking: Discussing the problems faced by computer users with different disabilities and the kinds of devices which help to overcome these problems
Reading: Reading to find specific information in a text
Writing: Writing an email summarizing different assistive technologies

Optional materials
Products designed for disabled computer users, or pictures of them

Plan

Teacher's activities	Students' activities	Comments
1 Assistive technology **A** Introduce the topic by directing SS' attention to the pictures. Read the vocabulary box with SS, focusing on the pronunciation of words such as *Braille* and *pneumatic*. Remind SS that they will not need all of the words in the box. **B** Elicit SS' answers and write a summary of SS' ideas on the board.	**A** In pairs, SS describe the pictures using the words from the box. **B** SS discuss the questions and make notes. SS then share their ideas with the rest of the class.	
2 Computers for the disabled **A** Monitor the task, helping with difficult words or structures. **B** Ask SS to complete the crossword with words from the text and compare their answers in pairs.	**A** SS read the article and find specific information. **B** SS solve the clues and complete the crossword.	This reading passage might be rather demanding for weaker SS. Refer SS to the Glossary or a dictionary for difficult terms such as *emboss, virtual keyboard, sip and puff, eyegaze system,* etc.

3 Language work: noun phrases

A Refer SS to the HELP box, making sure they understand what a noun phrase is and the function and types of modifiers.

B If SS are struggling with this task, have them write their answers in pairs first and then check answers with the whole class.

A SS decide what type of modifier is placed before the head in the noun phrases.

B SS then explain the noun phrases as in the example.

4 Assistive technologies for the blind

A Read through the unfinished notes with the SS. Play track 13 of the CD all the way through for SS to take notes.

B Let SS compare notes in pairs. Play the CD again, pausing if necessary. Ask SS to check their answers and complete the notes.

A SS listen and make notes about the topics.

B In pairs, SS help each other to improve their notes and then listen again to check their answers.

You may like to give SS a copy of the audio script.

5 Investing in assistive technologies

You may like to set this task for homework; however, if done in class, monitor the task, helping where needed. If you have access to the Internet in class, encourage SS to find suppliers of assistive technologies in your area or country.

SS write an email to their director of studies / manager summarizing the different assistive technologies available and the kind of people they can help.

Some SS may like to visit some websites about assistive technology or the WAI (Web Accessibility Initiative). Encourage them to use Google in English to find appropriate sites.

Online task

Visit www.cambridge.org/elt/ict for an online task related to the topic of this module.

Evaluation of the unit:

Answer key

1 Assistive technology

A

Possible answers

In picture a, a blind student is using an adapted keyboard in the presence of his tutor. The headphones and a screen reader program allow him to hear the text from the screen.

In picture b, a blind girl is using a screen magnifier, a type of software that enlarges text and images appearing on the screen.

In picture c, a motor-impaired person (probably someone with quadriplegia) is using a pneumatic switch - known as a sip and puff – to operate the computer.

In picture d, a motor-impaired user is unable to type on a standard keyboard. The on-screen keyboard is activated by the user's eyes when he pauses on the virtual keys for a few seconds. The video camera and special software determine the eye's gazepoint on the screen.

B

Possible answers

1 The main limitation experienced by blind users is the inability to see the screen. In addition, they cannot read printed documents, office correspondence, etc. Users with partial vision cannot see small character sizes on the screen. There are various degrees of mobility limitation; most motor-impaired users are not able to use a standard keyboard and have difficulty in manipulating computer devices and printed material.

2 For blind users, devices include Braille input devices, speech synthesis systems, scanners (with Optical Character Recognition), Braille printers (embossers), etc.

3 There are adapted keyboards designed for people with different kinds of mobility limitations; there are a variety of alternative input devices that produce and transmit keystrokes as if generated by the keyboard, for example muscle switches, optical head pointers, speech recognition devices, systems that scan the movements of the eye or the head in order to make selections on the computer screen, etc.

2 Computers for the disabled

A

1 The Americans with Disabilities Act (ADA); the Disability Discrimination Act

2 He uses an adapted keyboard, headphones and screen reading software.

3 Electronic notetakers

4 Optical Character Recognition (OCR)

5 The eyegaze system

6 The pneumatic switch, also known as a *sip and puff*

7 Voice recognition devices understand human speech, allowing users to speak to the computer and input data.

B

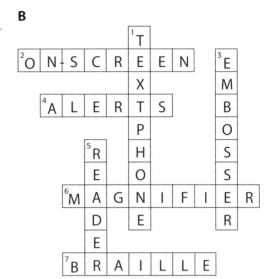

3 Language work: noun phrases

A

1a   2d   3c   4a   5a   6b

B

2 An engineer who works in rehabilitation (using technology to improve the quality of life for people with disabilities)

3 Abilities that the employee has

4 A keyboard that has been adapted

5 A computer that is activated by voice

6 A device that points (used to move the pointer on the screen)

4 Assistive technologies for the blind

A and B

1 A project for blind workers: studying each person's needs and then finding equipment for them

2 Braille devices, speech synthesis systems, scanners, voice recognition systems

3 Voice recognition allows users to control the computer by voice; speech synthesis reads the output from the screen in synthetic speech.

4 To make web pages accessible to all users, especially people with disabilities

5 Microsoft and Apple include support in their operating systems; Compaq has DECtalk Express, a speech synthesizer; IBM has ViaVoice (speech recognition software); GW Micro offers Small-Talk Ultra, a talking computer

5 Investing in assistive technologies

Open task

Audio script

Interviewer: Mr Hartley, can you tell us what you're working on at the moment?

Mike: Right now we're working with a group of blind employees here in Washington. We're studying each person's needs and abilities, and then we're going to find or design equipment for them.

Interviewer: What types of technology do blind users find helpful?

Mike: Well, a blind person needs to interact with the computer in some way, and Braille devices and speech synthesis systems are very useful ways of enabling them to do this, as are scanners and voice recognition systems.

Interviewer: What's the difference between voice recognition and speech synthesis?

Mike: Well, voice recognition systems let the user instruct the computer verbally – by talking. Speech synthesis systems allow the computer to communicate with the user by reading the output from the screen in synthetic speech.

Interviewer: Is it easy for blind users to access information on the Web?

Mike: Well, that depends on how the website is designed. Today, web designers are starting to follow the standards and guidelines developed by the Web Accessibility Initiative.

Interviewer: What's the goal of the Web Accessibility Initiative?

Mike: It tries to make web pages accessible to all users, especially those with disabilities. They encourage designers to use techniques that help disabled users understand, navigate, and interact with the Web. For example, they recommend providing audio descriptions as well as text, or to use Cascading Style Sheets that can include oral presentations.

Interviewer: Are big companies involved in producing assistive technologies?

Mike: Yes. Microsoft Windows and Apple Mac OS support screen magnifiers, text-to-speech, talking alerts, etc. Compaq has DECtalk Express, a speech synthesizer that lets you hear what is displayed on the screen. IBM has ViaVoice, which is speech recognition software. GW Micro has a full-featured talking computer called Small-Talk Ultra, which also includes a screen reader for the blind, Wi-Fi, Bluetooth and USB.

3 Storage devices

Learning objectives

In this module, you will:

- learn about different types of magnetic drives and disks.
- give instructions and advice on how to protect data.
- use technical vocabulary associated with optical storage devices and media.
- learn and use more discourse connectors.
- learn about the technical details of flash memory and its uses.
- learn different ways of making new words – affixation, conversion and compounding.
- describe flash-based devices.

Topics

Magnetic storage devices and media (floppy disks, hard drives, portable hard drives, tape drives)

Care and handling of disks

Learning objectives

To discriminate between different types of magnetic drive and disk

To give instructions and advice on how to protect data

Language

Grammar: The imperative and *should/shouldn't* to explain precautions and give warnings

Vocabulary: *magnetic, floppy disk, C: drive, tape, portable hard drive, read/write head, spin, platter, format, track, sector, directory, partition, back up, seek time, millisecond, data transfer rate, fragmentation, defragmentation*

Skills

Listening: Listening for specific information in a conversation

Speaking: Discussing what you should do to protect your data

Reading: Understanding technical details

Writing: Writing an email explaining hard drive precautions.

Optional materials

Real storage media, e.g. a diskette and/or a portable hard drive

Plan

Teacher's activities	Students' activities	Comments
Module page You may want to point out the learning objectives for your SS. You may also like to ask these introductory questions: *What are storage devices? What do they do?*	SS familiarize themselves with the topics and objectives of the Module. SS answer the questions and note any new vocabulary.	The Glossary in the Student's Book contains a definition of 'storage device'.
1 Types of magnetic drive **A** You may like to show SS real examples of disks and drives (e.g. old floppies, a magnetic tape, a portable hard drive, etc.). **B** Monitor the task, helping where needed. This task practises key words from the descriptions in A.	**A** SS look at the pictures and descriptions and find the required information. **B** SS complete the gaps with words from the box.	**Dis<u>k</u>** refers to magnetic storage media (e.g. a hard disk) **Dis<u>c</u>** refers to optical media (e.g. CD, DVD, etc.) The terms *hard drive, hard disk,* and *hard disk drive* refer to the same thing. However, strictly speaking, *hard drive* refers to the entire unit containing the disks (platters), the read/write heads and the motors. Optical storage is looked at in Unit 11.

2 Buying a portable hard drive

    A Play track 14 of the CD and ask SS the question: *Does she buy anything?*

    B Read the questions with SS first and then play the CD again, pausing if necessary.

    A SS listen to the conversation and answer the question.

    B SS listen again and answer the questions.

You may like to give SS a copy of the audio script after the task and ask them to read the dialogue aloud in pairs.

3 Magnetic storage

    A, **B** and **C**

    Monitor these tasks, helping with technical details if necessary.

    A SS read the text and then identify a track and a sector in the illustration.

    B SS decide if the sentences are true or false. SS then correct the false sentences, using information from the text.

    C SS match some key words from the text with the correct definitions.

Make sure SS understand these basic concepts: *formatting*, *tracks* and *sectors*, *partition*, *back up*, *seek time* versus *data transfer rate*. Refer SS to the Glossary if necessary.

4 Language work: precautions

    A Refer SS to the HELP box, explaining the use of the imperative to give warnings and instructions.

    B Refer SS to the HELP box again, explaining the use of *should/ shouldn't* in this context. Provide more examples if necessary. Monitor the task, checking that SS are using *should/shouldn't* correctly.

    A SS match the instructions to the pictures.

    B In pairs, SS discuss what we should or shouldn't do to protect our data.

You may also like to remind SS that *must* is used to express obligation and *mustn't* prohibition.

5 Word building

    Encourage SS to keep records of technical words according to word-building criteria – that is, recording words by word families. Explain that word families are often formed by adding prefixes and suffixes to the root word.

    SS decide if the words in the boxes are nouns, verbs, adjectives or adverbs. SS then choose the appropriate words to complete the sentences.

6 Explaining hard drive precautions

    Read the rubric with the SS, explaining *head crash* again if necessary. You may like to set this task for homework.

    SS write a reply to a friend's email explaining why a head crash may have happened and the precautions she should take to avoid it happening again.

A *head crash* occurs when the read/write head of a hard disk drive touches its rotating disk (platter), resulting in damage to its magnetic surface.

Answer key

1 Types of magnetic drive

A

1 C: drive
2 A portable external hard drive
3 Magnetic tape drive
4 3.5"; 1.44MB

B

1 storage
2 capacity
3 hold
4 secondary
5 archiving

2 Buying a portable hard drive

A

No, she doesn't buy anything.

B

1 160 gigabytes
2 12 gigabytes
3 The Iomega eGO
4 £68
5 £55

3 Magnetic storage

A

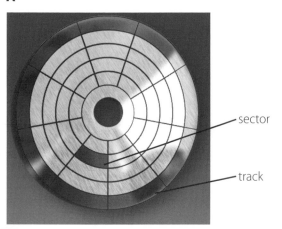

sector

track

B

1 False – A hard drive spins **more quickly than** a floppy disk drive.
2 True
3 False – Hard drives **can** be partitioned to run separate operating systems on the same disk.
4 False – *Seek time* and *transfer rate* mean **different things**. *Seek time* **is the average time it takes the read/write heads to move and find data;** *transfer rate* **is the average speed required to transmit data from the disk to the CPU.**
5 True

C

1d   2a   3b   4e   5c

4 Language work: precautions

A

1b   2d   3e   4a   5f   6c

B

1 **Update / You should update** your anti-virus program regularly, …
2 **Store / You should store** your discs in a protective case.
3 **Use / You should use** passwords and security devices …
4 **Don't write / You shouldn't write** on discs with permanent marker pens.
5 **Insert / You should insert** the disc into the disc drive carefully.
6 **Don't leave / You shouldn't leave** floppies or hard drives near magnets; …

5 Word building

magnet *n*
magnetism *n*
magnetic *adj*
magnetize *v*
magnetically *adv*
magnetized *adj* or *past participle of verb*

1 Magnetism
2 magnetic
3 magnetized

fragment *n* or *v*
defragmenter *n*
fragmentation *n*
fragmented *adj* or *past participle of verb*

4 fragmented
5 Fragmentation
6 defragmenter

6 Explaining hard drive precautions

Possible answer

Hard drives are very sensitive to vibrations and shocks. A head crash may occur when the read/write head of a hard disk drive touches its rotating disk (platter). This can scratch and damage the disk surface.

To avoid this kind of problem, you should take some precautions:

*   Don't hit or move the computer while it is operating.
*   You shouldn't turn your PC on and off quickly. Wait a few seconds to ensure that the hard drive has stopped spinning.
*   You should back up your hard drive regularly. To make copies of your important files, you can use a backup utility (sometimes included with the operating system) or you can use the *Copy* and *Paste* commands to transfer files to another storage device (for instance, an external hard drive, a DVD-RW disc or a pen drive).

Audio script

Sue: I'm looking for a portable hard drive. Have you got any?

Assistant: Sure. If you come with me, I'll show you some drives over here.

Sue: What different systems are there?

Assistant: At the moment we've got two products that might interest you: the Iomega eGO portable hard drive, which can store 160 gigabytes, and the Edge DiskGO mini portable hard drive, which can store 12 gigabytes.

Sue: So the Iomega model can hold a lot more information. Would you recommend it?

Assistant: Well, not necessarily. It all depends on your needs. The Iomega is more for mobile professionals, as it's big enough to back up your entire PC. The Edge Drive, on the other hand, is ultra lightweight, so it's ideal for transporting personal files like photos, music and data files.

Sue: I see. And how much do they cost?

Assistant: The Iomega eGO costs £68 and the Edge DiskGO is £55.

Sue: Right. Thanks very much. I think I need to think about it.

Optical storage

Topic
Optical discs (CD, DVD, HD-DVD and Blu-ray) and drives

Learning objectives
To develop listening and reading skills by recognizing the most relevant information in a text

To acquire technical vocabulary associated with optical storage devices and media

To recognize and use discourse connectors

Language
Grammar: Discourse cohesion: connectors

Vocabulary: *optical drive, laser beam, DVD burner, portable DVD player, dual/double layer, backward-compatible, Blu-ray disc*
Abbreviations: *CD-ROM, CD-R, CD-RW, DVD-ROM, DVD-R, DVD-RW, HD-DVD*

Skills
Listening: Understanding specific information in a conversation and correcting false statements

Speaking: Discussing the pros and cons of using different storage devices for particular purposes

Reading: Finding technical specs, formats and uses of different optical media in a text
Making notes on a text
Analysing the function of linking words in a text

Writing: Posting a comment on an online forum

Optional materials
A CD, a DVD and a Blu-ray disc

Plan

Teacher's activities	Students' activities	Comments
1 CDs and DVDs **A** Monitor the discussions, noting any vocabulary problems that arise. Do not give the answer for Task A yet, as SS will listen for it in Task C. **B** If you do not speak your SS' mother tongue, ask them to explain the terms in English. **C** Play track 15 of the CD and then check answers to A. **D** Play the CD again and then correct the false sentences on the board.	**A** In pairs, SS discuss the questions. **B** SS translate the expressions into their own language. **C** SS listen to the conversation at a computer shop and check their answers to A. **D** SS listen again and decide whether the sentences are true or false. SS then correct the false ones.	To introduce the unit, you may like to show some different optical media (e.g. a CD, DVD and Blu-ray disc). **A** and **B** are designed as warm-up activities to pre-teach some vocabulary and prepare SS for the listening task.
2 Optical discs and drives **A** Monitor the task, helping with technical details and drawing SS' attention to the pictures. Refer SS to the Glossary if necessary. **B** You may like to draw the table on the board and summarize the technical details of the different optical media: capacity, formats and uses.	**A** SS read the text and find the specific information required. SS can then compare their answers with a partner. **B** SS read the text again and make notes about the features of CDs, DVDs and Blu-ray discs.	Make sure that SS understand the technical differences between CDs and DVDs, and the different formats. Refer SS to the Glossary if necessary.

3 Language work: connectors 2 **A** Remind SS of the work they did on connectors in Unit 8, emphasizing that awareness of connectors can help them to develop their reading and writing skills. You may like to draw the table on the board. **B** and **C** Refer SS to the HELP box, providing more examples if necessary. Encourage SS to use dictionaries if necessary.	**A** SS look at some extracts from the texts and put the connectors into the correct columns. **B** SS look at the HELP box, check answers to A and translate the connectors. **C** SS choose the correct connectors to complete the sentences.	You may like to refer SS back to the HELP box on connectors in Unit 8.
4 Choosing storage devices Tell SS that this is a good opportunity to practise connectors for expressing contrast and adding ideas. Ask SS to justify their choices.	In pairs or small groups, SS look at the list of products and choose the most suitable storage device for different purposes.	Accept different answers as long as they are justified.
5 Format wars Explain that people often post messages on forums or blogs about certain topics. You may like to set this task for homework.	SS read three posts from a forum about the topic *Blu-ray versus HD-DVD* and then write their own response, giving their opinion on the topic.	Weaker SS may need help with grammar and vocabulary. Encourage SS to use dictionaries if necessary.

Evaluation of the unit:

Answer key

1 CDs and DVDs

A

1 CD stands for *compact disc*; DVD stands for *digital versatile disc*.
2 DVDs can hold more information than CDs. (A basic DVD can hold up to seven times more data than a compact disc.)

B

Open task

C

Students check their answers to A.

D

1 True
2 False – The dimensions of a CD and a DVD are 1.**2** mm thick and **12** cm in diameter.
3 True
4 False – A basic DVD can hold **4**.7 gigabytes.
5 False – You need a **DVD player** or a **DVD computer drive** to read DVDs.
6 True
7 False – A DVD-writer **is compatible** with old CD-ROMs.

2 Optical discs and drives

A

1 Optical discs can store data at much higher densities than magnetic disks; they are therefore ideal for multimedia applications where images, animation and sound occupy a lot of disc space. Furthermore, they are not affected by magnetic fields. This means that they are secure and stable – for example, they can be transported through airport metal detectors without damaging the data. However, optical drives are slower than hard drives.

2 17GB

3 A DVD burner is a DVD computer drive that records data on DVDs. A DVD recorder typically refers to a stand-alone unit, similar to a video cassette recorder.

4 multi-format playback

5 HD-DVD and Blu-ray

6 Unlike DVDs, which use a red laser to read/write data, Blu-ray uses a blue-violet laser.

B

CDs
Capacity
650–700 MB

Formats
CD-ROMs (**r**ead-**o**nly **m**emory) are 'read-only' units, meaning you cannot change the data stored on them (for example, a dictionary or a game).
CD-R (**r**ecordable) discs are write-once devices which let you duplicate music CDs and other data CDs.
CD-RW (**rew**ritable) discs enable you to write onto them many times, just like a hard drive.

Possible uses
CD-ROM: to include a dictionary or a game
CD-R: to duplicate music and data CDs
CD-RW: to back up important files

DVDs
Capacity
A basic DVD can hold 4.7GB. A DVD can also be double-sided, dual layer, with a capacity of 17GB.

Formats
DVD-ROMs are used in DVD computer drives. They allow for data archiving as well as interactive content (for example, an encyclopedia or a movie).
DVD-R or DVD+R can only be recorded on once.
DVD-RW or DVD+RW discs can be erased and reused many times. They are used to back up data files and to record audio and video.

Possible uses
DVD-ROM: to sell interactive content (for example, an encyclopedia, a movie, etc.)
DVD-R: to back up information
DVD-RW: to back up data files and to record audio and video

Blu-ray discs
Capacity
25GB (single layer), 50GB (dual layer) and 100GB (four layer)

Formats
Not mentioned in text

Possible uses
To record and play high-definition TV, audio and computer data

3 Language work: connectors 2

A

Indicating addition	Making contrasts	Explaining the results or effects of something
Furthermore	However	Therefore
In addition	Whereas	As a result

B

Open task

C

1 Although

2 As a result

3 so

4 because

5 and

6 therefore

4 Choosing storage devices

Possible answers

1 Seagate hard drive

2 Panasonic portable DVD player

3 Seagate hard drive; Iomega portable hard drive; Toshiba USB flash drive

4 Iomega portable hard drive; LaCie DVD drive

5 Seagate hard drive; LaCie DVD drive

6 Sony Blu-ray disc drive

5 Format wars

Open task

Audio script

Paul: Hi. I need to buy some blank discs, but I'm not sure whether to buy CDs or DVDs. What's the difference?

Assistant: OK, I'll explain. CD stands for compact disc, as you probably know, and DVD is short for digital versatile disc. A DVD is a type of optical disc technology used for storing movies, music and data. It's made from polycarbonate plastic coated with an aluminium layer, but that's probably more information than you need!

Paul: So, what's the difference between them?

Assistant: Well, they look the same and both are 1.2 mm thick and 12 cm in diameter. Both technologies use a laser beam to read the digital data encoded on the disc. But they differ in internal structure and capacity. The major difference is that a DVD has a greater data capacity. A CD usually has a capacity of 650 megabytes, while the smallest capacity you'll find on a DVD is 4.7 gigabytes.

Paul: And do you need a special drive to read and write data onto DVD, or can I use my CD drive?

Assistant: No, you need a DVD player or a DVD computer drive.

Paul: And what sort of information can a DVD hold?

Assistant: It depends on the type of DVD. DVD-Video discs contain films, including the video content, soundtracks in different languages, and subtitles. DVD-Audio discs contain high-definition sound, and DVD-Data discs contain computer data. Of course, a DVD can contain any combination of video, audio and data content.

Paul: And what about my old CDs? Can I use a DVD drive to play different types of CDs?

Assistant: Yeah – one of the best features of new DVD Writers is that they are backward-compatible, which means they can play old CDs and CD-ROMs as well as DVDs.

Photocopiable © Cambridge University Press 2008

Topic

Flash memory (cards, drives and media players)

Learning objectives

To understand the technical details of flash memory and its uses

To understand different ways of making new words: affixation, conversion and compounding

To be able to describe flash-based devices

Language

Grammar: Word formation (prefixes, suffixes, conversion, compounds)

Vocabulary: *flash memory card, USB flash drive, pen drive, non-volatile, card reader, hybrid hard drive*

Skills

Listening: Listening for specific information in a conversation at a consumer electronics show

Speaking: Describing flash drives and MP3/MP4 players

Reading: Understanding specific information from a text about flash memory and its uses

Writing: Writing a reply to an SMS message

Optional materials

Real flash-based devices, for example: memory cards from cameras or mobiles; USB flash drives with different designs and capabilities; an MP4 player

Plan

Teacher's activities	Students' activities	Comments
1 Flash-based gadgets Monitor the task, noting any vocabulary problems that arise.	SS match the descriptions to the pictures illustrating flash-based devices.	To introduce the unit, you may like to show SS some real flash devices (e.g. the flash memory card from a digital camera, a USB drive, etc.). SS should be able to distinguish between hard drives, DVDs and Flash memory. Refer SS to the Glossary if necessary.
2 Memory in a Flash! **A** Draw the SS' attention to the title of the text and ask SS the question: *Why is it a suitable title for the article?* Check the answers once SS have read the first paragraph. **B** and **C** Monitor the tasks, helping with technical details if necessary.	**A** SS answer the question and then read the first paragraph to find out. **B** SS read the article and answer the questions. **C** SS find words or phrases in the text corresponding to the definitions.	There are three key words when defining Flash memory: *non-volatile, erasable* and *solid-state* (it has no moving parts). Make sure SS understand these terms, referring them to the Glossary if necessary.

3 Language work: word building **A** Refer SS to the HELP box, explaining that affixation, conversion and compounding will help them develop their vocabulary. You may like to write more examples of compounds on the board, e.g. *video console, smartcard, cell phone (AmE), smartphone, broadband*. **B** This is an opportunity to practise what SS have learnt about word formation.	**A** SS first study word formation processes and then make words from *blog*, *mail* and *print*. **B** SS choose the correct word to complete an authentic review of a flash-based voice recorder.	Prefixes often change the meaning of the root word. Suffixes change the class of the root word; they tell you if it is a noun, a verb, an adjective or an adverb. Compounds work as a single word; however, they should not be confused with collocations, which are two or more words that often appear together.
4 Describing flash drives **A** Play track 16 of the CD and ask SS the question: *Which product is the visitor most interested in?* **B** Draw the table on the board. Play the CD again. **C** Play the CD a third time. You may like to pause after each question-answer exchange. **D** Refer SS to the *Useful language* box. Monitor the discussions, helping where needed. **E** Help SS with any vocabulary and technical queries. SS should write very concise answers, as they would in a real text message.	**A** SS listen and decide which product the visitor is most interested in. **B** SS listen again and tick the features mentioned for each device. **C** SS listen again and answer the questions. **D** In pairs, SS describe their own flash device(s). **E** SS write a reply to a text from a friend asking about the difference between MP3 and MP4 players.	Salespeople often describe products to potential customers at consumer electronic shows. You may like to give SS a copy of the audio script. You may like to refer SS to the chat abbreviations in Unit 18, which are also useful for writing text messages SS will probably already know a lot of about MP3 and MP4 players.
5 Vocabulary revision You may like to set this task for homework or as an information gap speaking activity.	SS solve the clues and complete the crossword, individually or in pairs	This task recycles vocabulary connected with the units in Module 3.

Evaluation of the unit:

Answer key

1 Flash-based gadgets

a3   b6   c5   d2   e1   f4

2 Memory in a flash!

A

Memory in a flash literally means 'very quick memory'. It is a suitable name for the text because the text is about flash drives, so called because they can be erased very quickly, or 'in a flash'.

B

1 A type of non-volatile memory that can be electronically erased and reprogrammed.
2 RAM is volatile; flash memory is non-volatile, so it retains its content when the power is turned off; RAM is faster.
3 They can store more that one bit per cell.
4 Flash drives are more easily transported than external hard drives; as they use solid-state technology, they don't have fragile moving parts that can break if dropped; however, they have less capacity than hard drives.
5 You can store both applications and data; applications can run on the host computer without requiring installation.
6 From 8MB to several gigabytes
7 The Memory Stick

C

1 non-volatile
2 rewritable
3 partitions
4 to back up
5 offloaded
6 flash card reader
7 hybrid

3 Word building

A

Possible answers

blog	mail	print
blogger	to mail	printout
to blog	mailing	to print
blogging	email	reprint
blogosphere	emailing	printer
photoblog	mailbox	printing
videoblog (vlog)	webmail (Hotmail)	printed
moblog	mailman	printable
weblog	mail merge	fingerprint
	mail order	footprint
	junk mail	printout
	snail mail	print head
		print spooler

B

1 lightweight
2 recording
3 playback
4 folders
5 activation
6 connector
7 download
8 storage

4 Describing flash drives

A

b

B

Features	Dragon flash drive	Dragon MP4 player
Back up computer data	✔	☐
Transport files between PCs	✔	☐
Audio and video playback	☐	✔
FM radio tuner	☐	✔
Voice recorder	☐	✔
Games	☐	✔

C

1 16GB
2 You just plug it into a USB port
3 It is more durable than a DVD drive or a hard drive (because there are no moving parts) and it's smaller.
4 Because they can play files in the MPEG-4 format.
5 2.7"
6 28 hours

D and **E**

Open tasks

5 Vocabulary revision

Audio script

Visitor: Hello there. I'm thinking of buying a USB flash drive and I've heard you're presenting a new device at this show. Could I see it?

Salesperson: Of course. This is the new Dragon flash drive, a compact flash memory drive that acts like a portable hard drive.

Visitor: And what's the storage capacity?

Salesperson: Well, this model here can hold 16 gigabytes of data. We also have drives of 64 gigs, but they're more expensive. The drive consists of a USB connector covered by a removable cap, a mass storage controller, and a flash memory chip. It also includes a write-protect switch and password protection.

Visitor: You're getting a bit too technical for me! Does it connect like a normal drive?

Salesperson: Yes, you just plug it into a USB port on your computer. You can copy files to and from it, just as you would do with any other drive.

Visitor: So what's the advantage of using a flash drive instead of a DVD or an external hard drive, then?

Salesperson: Good question. Firstly, a flash drive is more durable because it doesn't contain any internal moving parts. Secondly, it's small enough to fit on your key ring or in your pocket. That makes it ideal for moving documents between home and the office, carrying music files, or backing up important documents.

Visitor: And what about music and video? Have you got any devices that can play that kind of thing?

Salesperson: Yes, we're also introducing the new Dragon MP4 player at the convention. It comes with 64 gigabytes of capacity, ideal for video fans.

Visitor: Er, sorry, what exactly is an MP4 player? Is it the same as an MP3 player?

Salesperson: Almost. It's a portable media player that plays files compressed in the MPEG-4 format, which is more efficient than MP3. This model also features a 2.7 inch colour screen, 28 hours of rechargeable battery life, and it supports multiple formats.

Visitor: OK. And what can you do with it?

Salesperson: Apart from the typical functions of a flash drive, you can also play movies, watch TV, listen to FM radio stations, record yourself and even play games.

Visitor: That sounds great. It might be just what I'm after! How much is it?

Photocopiable © Cambridge University Press 2008

4 Basic software

Learning objectives

In this module, you will:

- learn about the function of the operating system.
- learn about the features of a graphical user interface, or GUI.
- practise using the correct determiners with countable and uncountable nouns.
- learn how to summarize a written text.
- learn about the basic features and applications of word processors.
- learn how to give and follow instructions.
- study the basic features and applications of spreadsheets and databases.
- practise forming and pronouncing plurals.

The operating system (OS)

Topics	Skills

Topics

Operating systems (Windows Vista, Linux, the Mac OS)
The graphical user interface (GUI)

Learning objectives

To understand the function of the operating system
To recognize the features of a graphical user interface, or GUI
To use the correct determiners with countable and uncountable nouns
To summarize a written text

Language

Grammar: Countable and uncountable nouns
Determiners

Vocabulary: *system software, operating system, application software, multitasking, user interface, GUI, WIMP environment, user-friendly, desktop, window, icon, folder, menu bar, drop-down menu, scroll bar, dock*

Skills

Listening: Completing a fact file about Windows Vista from information given in an interview

Speaking: Comparing operating systems

Reading: Understanding specific information from a text
Guessing the meaning of words from context and translating them

Writing: A summary

Optional materials

Sample screenshots of a graphical user interface (e.g. Windows, Mac OS or Linux)

Technical help is given on page 64.

Plan

Teacher's activities	Students' activities	Comments
Module page You may want to point out the learning objectives for your SS.	SS familiarize themselves with the topics and objectives of the Module.	
1 The function of the operating system **A** and **B** Elicit answers from SS. You may like to draw the diagram from the Technical help on page 64 on the board, which can help SS understand and explain the function of the operating system.	**A** In pairs, SS answer the questions. **B** SS complete the text with words from the box.	It is assumed that SS have heard of operating systems before. Make sure SS understand the difference between the operating system and application software. Refer SS to the Glossary if necessary.

2 GUI operating systems

A Elicit answers from SS.

B Encourage SS to read the text quickly. They will be reading it in more detail in Task C.

C Monitor the task, helping with any vocabulary problems.

D Ask SS to refer back to the text and to translate the expressions into their own language.

E Monitor the task, helping with any vocabulary problems.

F If necessary, refer SS to the screenshots on page 65.

A In pairs, SS discuss the questions.

B SS read the text and decide which of the adjectives best describe a GUI.

C SS read the text again and then answer the questions.

D SS translate the words.

E SS label the interface features on the screenshot with words from the list.

F In pairs, SS compare the Mac OS user interface with a Windows or Linux interface.

The Mac screen illustrates a GUI; it is also intended to prepare SS for reading. A user-friendly operating system would mean the system functions are accessed by selecting self-explanatory icons and items from menus. A user-friendly interface is based on interactive and intuitive features.

Make sure SS understand these basic concepts: *user interface, user-friendly, a WIMP environment, desktop, nested folder, toolbar* and *multitasking*. Refer SS to the Glossary if necessary.

3 Windows Vista

A You may like to pre-teach key phrases like *Windows version, compatible with, security, firewall,* etc. Play track 17 of the CD.

B Play the CD again, pausing to allow SS to write their notes. Play the CD a third time if necessary.

A SS listen to the interview and answer the questions.

B SS listen again and complete the fact file. SS then compare their answers in pairs.

You may like to encourage SS to read more about Windows Vista on the Web.

4 Language work: countable and uncountable nouns

A Refer SS to the HELP box, providing some other examples of non-countable nouns in everyday English (e.g. *weather, luggage*).

B Refer SS back to the HELP box, which focuses on determiners (*the, a, an*).

A SS decide if the nouns are countable or uncountable.

B SS complete the text using *a, an, the* or nothing.

A contrastive analysis with SS' mother tongue may be useful here.

5 Writing a summary

You may like to set this task as homework.

SS follow the step-by-step instructions and write the summary.

Evaluation of the unit:

Answer key

1 The function of the operating system

A

1

Possible answers

Microsoft Windows, Mac OS from Apple, Linux, Unix, Windows Mobile (Pocket PC), Palm OS

2

Possible answer

The function of the operating system is to control the hardware and software resources. The OS consists of a set of programs that interface between the user, application programs and the computer.

B

1 software	3 application software
2 system software	4 operating system

2 GUI operating systems

A

1 User-friendly means *easy to use* or *designed with the user in mind*.
2 Open task

B

user-friendly, accessible, intuitive, graphics-based

C

1 text-based
2 The Macintosh was the first computer that used a mouse and a graphical user interface.
3 windows, icons, menus and pointer.
4 By double-clicking the program icon or a document icon.
5 Running several programs and doing various tasks at the same time.
6 Unix
7 Open-source software like Linux is freely distributed – i.e. you can copy, change and redistribute its code.
8 Windows Mobile

D

Open task

E

a menu bar
b drop-down (pull-down) menu
c program icon
d folder icon
e document icon
f window
g hard drive icon
h scroll bar
i desktop
j dock

F

Open task

3 Windows Vista

A

1 It's easy to use, it's based on graphic images, and it's compatible with thousands of programs.
2 Ultimate edition

B

1 Home Basic	6 anti-spyware
2 entertainment	7 internet attacks
3 business organizations	8 Microsoft Office
4 visual style	9 word processor
5 speech recognition	10 presentation graphics

4 Language work: countable and uncountable nouns

A

user *c*
email *c* and *u* (*c*: a message; *u*: the system for sending messages over the Net)
computing *u*
edition *c*
entertainment *u*
interface *c*
icon *c*
technology *c* and *u* (*c*: a type of technology – *Wi-Fi is a new technology*; *u*: technology in general – *Technology is advancing quickly*)
security *c* and *u* (*c*: in financial usage; *u*: meaning *safety*)
spyware *u*

B

1 an	3 The	5 a	7 –
2 a	4 –	6 a	8 –

5 Writing a summary

Possible answer

In the past, only experts used computers. Then, in the mid 1980s, Macs and PCs were designed with a graphic user interface to facilitate interaction with the computer. Today, all kinds of people use computers, so there is an emphasis on accessibility and user-friendly systems.

A GUI uses a WIMP environment (windows, icons, menus and pointer).

The most popular operating systems are Windows, Mac OS, Unix, Linux, and Windows Mobile for handheld devices.

Audio script

Interviewer: There is no doubt that Windows has revolutionized the way we use computers today. Bill, can you explain just why it's so popular?

Bill: Well, very simply, people find Windows very easy to use because everything is presented in graphic images. It's also compatible with thousands of programs.

Interviewer: The big news at the moment is, of course, the launch of Windows Vista – the successor to Windows XP. I understand that there are several versions of Vista available. Could you give us some advice on which one to get?

Bill: Yes, you're right – there are four main editions: Home Basic, Home Premium, Business and Ultimate. Home Basic is designed for users with basic needs, such as email and internet access. Home Premium is for more advanced home computing and entertainment. It includes a DVD maker, a movie maker and a Media Centre, which lets you listen to music, watch video and record TV programmes on your PC. The Business edition is ideal for business organizations of all sizes. It offers new backup technologies and advanced networking capabilities. Finally, the Ultimate edition combines all the features of the other editions, making it the most complete. It has everything you need to enjoy the latest in music, games, digital photography and high-definition TV. It's aimed at high-end PC users, gamers and multimedia professionals.

Interviewer: And what other factors make Windows Vista so attractive?

Bill: The user interface has been redesigned with new icons and a new visual style. The system gives you more flexibility when you search and organize your files, and it offers support for the latest technologies, from DVD creation to speech recognition.

Interviewer: What about internet connections? Have they been improved?

Bill: Yes, Internet Explorer is more reliable and secure. The Security Centre includes an anti-spyware program called Windows Defender and a firewall that protects your computer from internet attacks.

Interviewer: And what sort of application software can you use with Windows?

Bill: The most popular is still Microsoft Office, a suite that includes the word processor, Word, an email program, the Excel spreadsheet program, and the presentation graphics program, PowerPoint.

Technical help: The function of the operating system

Peripherals (printer, mouse, etc.)

Operating system

Computer (CPU, memory)

Application software (graphics, email, etc.)

User

Unit 14 | Word processing (WP)

Topic
Word processing

Learning objectives
To understand the basic features and applications of word processors
To give and follow instructions

Language
Grammar: Giving and following instructions: the use of the imperative, sequence words (*first, next, then, after that, finally*) and other expressions

Vocabulary: *menu bar, standard toolbar, formatting toolbar, header, footer, typeface, bold, italic, indent, drawing tools, align left, print preview, undo, columns, bullets, insert, table, hyperlink, edit, cut, paste, clipboard, spell checker, thesaurus, grammar checker*

Skills
Listening: Completing gaps in a conversation about how to move text in Word.

Speaking: Giving instructions on how to do particular tasks with a word processor

Reading: Matching descriptions with pictures
Finding sentences printed in the wrong position in a text and deciding where they should go

Writing: Writing instructions for using the *Find and Replace* command in Word

Optional materials
A word processor program and a computer

Plan

Teacher's activities	Students' activities	Comments
1 Word processing features **A** Go through the questions with the class. **B** Draw SS' attention to the screenshot, asking them to translate the terms into their own language. Teach SS how to pronounce the features illustrated and any menu or other commands they are interested in. **C** Monitor the task, helping with any vocabulary problems.	**A** In pairs, SS answer the questions and familiarize themselves with the topic. **B** SS look at the screenshot and translate the labelled features and functions. **C** SS complete sentences with the correct feature or function from **B**.	You may like to introduce the topic by showing a word processor on a computer. The screen shows a letter edited with *Microsoft Word*. Make sure SS understand the labelled features. They should also be able to distinguish the three bars at the top: the *Menu bar*, the *Standard Toolbar* and the *Formatting Toolbar*. Refer SS to the Glossary if necessary.
2 Word Sudoku Read the instructions on how to play Sudoko with the SS, giving additional explanations if necessary.	SS do a Word Sudoku.	This Sudoku is quite a challenge for SS and may take some time if they are not familiar with the type of puzzle. You may like to set this for homework.

3 The *Cut and Paste* technique

  A Direct SS' attention to the Edit menu. Play track 18 of the CD and ask SS the question:
    How many steps are involved in carrying out the Cut and Paste *task?*

  B Play the CD again. Play the CD a third time, pausing if necessary, and check answers. Then ask SS to read the dialogue aloud, in pairs.

  A SS first listen to two friends talking about how to move text in Word, and answer the question.

  B SS listen again and complete the dialogue with words from the box.

You may like to ask SS to translate the commands in the Edit menu.

4 Language work: giving and following instructions

  A Refer SS to the HELP box, and then ask them to correct the mistakes in the dialogue and to read the correct version aloud in pairs.

  B Monitor the task, helping with any vocabulary problems.

  C Monitor the task, helping where needed. You may like to set this task for homework.

  D Monitor the discussions, encouraging SS to use words and expressions from the HELP box.

  A SS correct six mistakes in a dialogue about how to insert a picture into a document.

  B SS complete the instructions on how to copy and paste in Word, using verbs from the box.

  C SS write instructions for using *Find and Replace,* based on the dialog box.

  D Students work in pairs: Student A gives instructions on how to create and save a document; Student B gives instructions on how to insert a picture from the Web into a Word document.

You may like to ask SS to translate the commands in the Insert Menu.

5 WP tools

  A and **B**
    Set these tasks at the same time. It is important that SS understand what they will be expected to do in Task B before they read the texts, otherwise they may find the texts confusing. Monitor the tasks, helping where needed.

  C You may like to provide some more example sentences with deliberate mistakes for SS to correct in a similar way.

  A SS read the descriptions of three WP tools and match them with the dialog boxes.

  B SS read through the descriptions, find three sentences printed in the wrong position and decide where they should go.

  C SS correct the three mistakes in a sentence and decide if they would be found by the spell checker or the grammar checker.

These tasks will help SS to learn about three useful writing tools: the spell checker, the thesaurus and the grammar checker.

Evaluation of the unit:

Answer key

1 Word processing features

A

Possible answers

1 A word processor is a computer program which manipulates text and produces documents suitable for printing.

2 A word processor can be used to compose, edit, format and print any sort of printable material. It is mainly used to write memos, briefs, technical reports and business letters. It also allows you to merge text from one file into another file; this is very useful for producing many files (e.g. personalized letters) with the same format but with different data.

3 Microsoft Word, Word Perfect, OpenOffice.org Writer, Kword. Word is probably the most popular, as it often comes ready-installed with Windows.

B

Open task

C

1 Toolbar; Formatting
2 typeface
3 Bold; Italic
4 Indent
5 Header; Footer

2 Word Sudoku

Insert Hyperlink	Drawing	Columns	Bullets	Undo	Open	🖼	☰	🔍
Align Left	Open	Print Preview	Insert Table	Insert Hyperlink	Columns	📷	📄	📋
Bullets	Insert Table	Undo	Drawing	Align Left	Print Preview	🖼	🎨	📋
Columns	Print Preview	Align Left	📋	📄	🎨	Insert Hyperlink	Insert Table	Undo
Drawing	Bullets	Insert Table	🎨	🔍	📷	Align Left	Open	Columns
Undo	Insert Hyperlink	Open	☰	🖼	🖼	Bullets	Print Preview	Drawing
🔍	🖼	🎨	Undo	Drawing	Align Left	Open	Bullets	Insert Table
🖼	☰	🎨	Columns	Open	Bullets	Print Preview	Undo	Insert Hyperlink
📋	📷	📄	Print Preview	Insert Table	Insert Hyperlink	Drawing	Columns	Align Left

3 The *Cut and Paste* technique

A

Four

B

1 First
2 Then
3 Like this
4 Now
5 right
6 Next
7 Finally
8 done that now
9 everything

4 Language work: giving and following instructions

A

A: I need a photo for my curriculum vitae. How do I insert one into this Word document?

B: Well, **first** choose *Insert* on the Menu bar.

A: **Like** this?

B: Yes. From the Insert menu, select *Picture*. As you can see, this displays a drop-down menu with different options: *Clip Art*, *From File*, *From Scanner*, *Chart*, etc. Select *From File* and you'll get a dialog box.

A: OK. I've done that now. What **next**?

B: OK. Now **you** navigate your hard drive's contents and find the picture that you want to insert.

A: Right. I'd like to include this one.

B: OK, good. Now click *Insert* and the photograph will be inserted into your document.

A: Here it is. Is that **right**?

B: Yes. **Finally**, right-click with the mouse and select *Format Picture* to adjust the size and other properties.

A: Brilliant, thanks!

B

1 select; drag
2 click
3 position
4 click; right-click

C

Possible answer

- First, click where you want to start searching for the text.
- Next, go to the Edit menu and select *Replace*. This displays a dialog box.
- As you can see in the illustration, you type the text you want to find (*computer programmer*) in the *Find what* box, and the new text (*software developer*) in the *Replace* box.
- To locate the first instance of the specified text, click *Replace*.
- Now you have two options: to replace all instances of the text, click *Replace All*; to move through the document and replace only specific instances, click *Find Next*. This is a safer option. Do not click *Replace All* unless you are certain that every instance of the text should be replaced.

D

Open task

5 WP tools

A

1c   2a   3b

B

1 Spell checkers can be used to compare words in the program's dictionary to those used in the user's document. The spell checker points out any words it cannot match, notifies the user, and allows them to make any changes; it even suggests possible correct spellings. **However, this does not mean that all the words in the document are spelled correctly.** ~~Like a conventional thesaurus, this database of words contains~~ ~~definitions and suggestions of words with similar and opposite meanings.~~ A word may be spelled correctly but still be wrong (*too* instead of *two*, for instance). This is a good first step at proofing a document because it can find many common errors, but users will still need to proofread documents to ensure complete accuracy.

2 Many word processors include an online thesaurus with which users can look up different words to use in similar instances. **Like a conventional thesaurus, this database of words contains definitions and suggestions of words with similar and opposite meanings.** ~~Their power comes not from knowing every grammatical rule, but from questioning the writer about certain parts of the text.~~ Some even include information about pronunciation and the history of a word.

3 Grammar checkers are applications that attempt to check more than just spelling. They count words in sentences to flag possible run-on sentences. They look for words that show possible conflicts between verbs and subjects and they offer advice about corrections. Grammar checkers are a step beyond spell checkers, but they are still not a substitute for a human editor. **Their power comes not from knowing every grammatical rule, but from questioning the writer about certain parts of the text.** ~~However, this does not mean that all the words in the document are spelled correctly.~~ They give the writer another chance to think about what he or she has written. The computer can alert writers to problems that wouldn't be obvious to them otherwise.

C

Mail merge combine**s** a form let**t**er with a database file to create customized cop**ies** of the letter.

The grammar checker would find the first mistake, the spell checker the second and third.

Audio script

Anna: Ben, do you know how I can move this paragraph? I want to put it at the end of this page.

Ben: Er … I think so. First, use the mouse to select the text you want to move. Then choose the *Cut* command from the Edit menu.

Anna: Like this?

Ben: Yes. The selected text disappears and goes onto the Clipboard. Now you find where you want the text to appear, and you click to position the insertion point there.

Anna: Mm, OK. Is that right?

Ben: Yes, if that's where you want it. Next, choose *Paste* from the Edit menu, or hold down *CTRL* and press *V*. Finally, check that the text has appeared in the right place.

Anna: OK, I've done that now. Is that everything?

Ben: Yes, that's it. If you make a mistake, you can choose *Undo* from the Edit menu, which will reverse your last editing command.

Anna: Brilliant! Thanks a lot.

Ben: That's OK, it's my pleasure.

Unit 15 | Spreadsheets and databases

Topics
The form and function of spreadsheet programs
Databases

Learning objectives
To understand the basic features and applications of spreadsheets and databases
To form and pronounce plurals correctly

Language
Grammar: Plurals
Vocabulary:
Spreadsheets: *column, row, cell, formula, value, chart, graph, invoice*
Databases: *DBMS, relational database, file, record, field, update, index, search, sort, query*

Skills
Listening: Listening for specific and general information in a lecture about spreadsheets
Speaking: Finding out about the software used by partner at home/work
Pronunciation of plurals
Reading: Understanding the basic features of databases and completing statements based on a text
Writing: Completing an invoice
Completing a business letter
Writing a fax of complaint

Optional materials
A real spreadsheet or database program

Plan

Teacher's activities	Students' activities	Comments
1 About spreadsheet programs **A** Elicit answers from SS but do not give the answer for Tasks A or B yet, as SS will listen for them in Task C. You might like to ask SS the question: *Have you ever used a spreadsheet? What for?* **B** Elicit answers from SS. Draw SS' attention to the caption explaining the terms *spreadsheet* and *worksheet*. **C** Play track 19 of the CD. SS check their answers to **A** and **B**. **D** Play the CD again, pausing if necessary. **E** Ask SS to justify their answers with information from the worksheet. **F** Teach different types of graphs and charts: *line, bar, pie chart,* etc.	**A** In pairs, SS discuss the questions. **B** SS look at the sample worksheet, label a *column*, a *row* and a *cell*, and answer the questions. **C** SS listen and check their answers to **A** and **B**. **D** SS listen again and correct the false sentences. **E** SS look at the worksheet and decide whether the sentences are true or false. **F** In pairs, SS discuss the advantages and disadvantages of showing information as a graph, rather than a spreadsheet.	You may like to show SS a real spreadsheet program on a laptop or PDA. The listening passage might be a little difficult for some SS, but the task is straightforward. If necessary, provide them with the audio script.

2 An invoice, a business letter and a fax

A Explain the difference between *invoice* and *bill*. Refer SS to a dictionary if necessary.

B Read through the business letter with SS, and draw their attention to the format and type of vocabulary.

C Refer SS to the *Useful language* box. Monitor the task, helping where needed.

A SS complete the invoice with words from the box. If possible, they generate a similar invoice outside class.

B SS complete the business letter that goes with the invoice.

C SS write a fax complaining about faulty hardware and software.

These activities could be set as a mini-project that SS can do on the computer. They can use a spreadsheet program like *Excel* to generate the invoice, and a word processor to write the fax.

3 Databases

A Elicit answers from SS and make a summary on the board.

B Use the picture to illustrate the difference between *file*, *record* and *field*. Do not give the answer for Task B yet, as SS will read for it in Task C.

C and D Monitor the tasks, helping with any vocabulary problems.

E Tell SS that all the terms in the puzzle appear in the text.

F Monitor the discussions, helping where needed. Alternative for homework: Ask SS to design a database form (on computer) for their music collection.

A In groups, SS make a list of applications for databases.

B SS look at the illustration of a database file and identify a *record* and a *field*.

C SS read the text and check answers to **B**.

D SS read the text again and complete the statements.

E SS solve the clues and complete the puzzle.

F In pairs, SS discuss what fields they would include in a database for a music collection

A database is: a file of structured data; a large collection of related information; an organized collection of data stored in a computer file.

You may like to compare an electronic database with a manual filing cabinet (e.g. a card index system) and ask SS what the advantages and disadvantages of each system are.

4 Language work: plurals

A Refer SS to the HELP box. Remind SS that the word *data* is a group noun (uncountable) and takes a third person singular when it refers to information processed by a computer: *The data **is** ready for processing*.

B Monitor the activity, and then read the words aloud for SS to check their answers.

A SS write the plural of the words.

B SS put the plurals into the correct columns and then listen to the teacher to check their answers.

Some SS may find it difficult to discriminate between the voiceless /s/ and the voiced /z/.

5 Software at home and at work

Refer SS to the *Useful language* box and monitor the discussions, helping where needed.

Online task

Visit www.cambridge.org/elt/ict for an online task related to the topic of this module.

In pairs, SS find out as much as they can about the software their partner uses at home or at work.

Ask SS to make a table in their notebook and complete it:

Software	Student A	Student B
Spreadsheet		
Database		
Word processor		
Videoconferencing		
Business accounting		
Email		
Web browser		

Evaluation of the unit:

Answer key

1 Spreadsheets and databases

A

Possible answers

1 A spreadsheet is like a large sheet of paper with a lot of columns and rows.
2 Spreadsheets are used in business for financial planning, to make calculations, to keep a record of the company's accounts, etc.

B

a column
b cell
c row

1 You can enter text, numbers and formulae (or formulas).
2 The values of the spreadsheet are automatically recalculated.

C

Students check their answers to A and B.

D

1 True
2 False – In a spreadsheet you can enter **text**, numbers and formulae.
3 False – You **can** change the width of columns.
4 True
5 False – Spreadsheets **can** be used as databases.

E

1 True
2 False – It's the result of adding cells B2, B3 and B4.
3 True

F

Possible answer

Charts and graphs assist in the interpretation of data. From the graph the reader can immediately compare the 2007 and 2008 figures and can also compare the different kinds of revenue and expenses.

2 An invoice, a business letter and a fax

A

1 Company
2 Product
3 Description
4 Quantity
5 Price
6 VAT
7 Grand total

B

1   Dear Ms Atkinson
2   I am writing to
3   I am enclosing
4   We would be grateful if you could
5   Please contact us
6   Yours sincerely

C

Possible answer

I am writing to complain about two products we received from your company last week.

The laser printer gives continuous error messages when we try to print out our documents. For some unknown reason, the printer doesn't work at all. In addition, I am unable to install the database program successfully on the hard drive. We find this unacceptable.

Please send us a new printer and an upgraded version of the database. We would also accept a full refund of the cost.

Yours sincerely,

R. Atkinson

3 Databases

A

Possible answers

To keep records or mailing lists with names, addresses, phone numbers, salaries, departments, etc.; to keep track of stock, sales, orders, bills and other financial information; to store and find information about patients in a hospital or general medical practice; to keep records of students/pupils at college/school; to store data about a music collection, with artist names, song titles, video clips, etc.; to catalogue books, CDs and DVDs in a library, or to record the books that readers borrow.

B

In the illustration there are four separate *records*.
Each record has eight *fields* (name, address, etc.). The photograph may be another field.

C

Students check their answers to B.

D

1   A database management system is used to **store, organize and retrieve information from a database**.
2   Information is entered on a database via **fields**.
3   Each field holds **a separate piece of information**.
4   *Updating* a file means **making changes, adding new records or deleting old ones**.
5   Some advantages of a database program over a manual filing system are: **it is much faster to consult; it occupies much less space; records can be easily sorted; information can be easily updated; computer databases can be shared by a lot of users over a network**.
6   Access to a common database over a network can be protected by using **user-defined passwords and other security devices**.

E

```
1  d  a  t  a  b  a  s  e
            2  r  e  c  o  r  d
                  3  f  i  e  l  d
         4  r  e  l  a  t  i  o  n  a  l
            5  n  e  t  w  o  r  k
            6  s  e  a  r  c  h
            7  s  o  r  t
            8  q  u  e  r  y
```

F

Possible answer

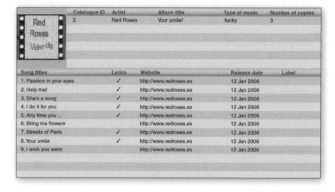

4 Language work: plurals

A

1 clients
2 keys
3 queries
4 businessmen
5 faxes
6 salaries
7 mice
8 viruses

B

/s/	/ɪz/	/z/
laptops	databases	passwords
graphs	switches	orders
networks	taxes	tables
spreadsheets	packages	systems

5 Software at home and at work

Open task

Audio script

OK, everyone. Let's begin with the basics. A spreadsheet program is normally used in business for financial planning – to keep a record of accounts, to analyse budgets or to make specific calculations. It's like a large piece of paper divided into columns and rows. Each column is labelled with a letter and each row is labelled with a number. The point where a column and a row intersect is called a cell. For example, you can have cells A1, B6, C5, and so on.

A cell can hold three types of information: text, numbers and formulae. For example, in this sample worksheet, the word *Sales* has been keyed into cell A2, and the values 890, 487 and 182 have been entered into cells B2, B3 and B4 respectively. So, when the formula B2+B3+B4 is keyed into cell B5, the program automatically calculates and displays the result.

Formulae are functions or operations that add, subtract, multiply or divide existing values to produce new values. We can use them to calculate totals, percentages or discounts.

When you change the value of one cell, the values in other cells are automatically recalculated. You can also update the information in different worksheets by linking cells. This means that when you make a change in one worksheet, the same change is made in the other worksheet.

The format menu in a spreadsheet usually includes several commands allowing you to choose the font, number alignment, borders, column width, and so on.

Most spreadsheet programs can also generate graphic representations. The value of cells are shown in different ways, such as line graphs, bar or pie charts. There are even three-dimensional options.

Some spreadsheet programs also have a database facility which transforms the values of the cells into a database. In this case, each column is a field and each row is a record.

Photocopiable © Cambridge University Press 2008

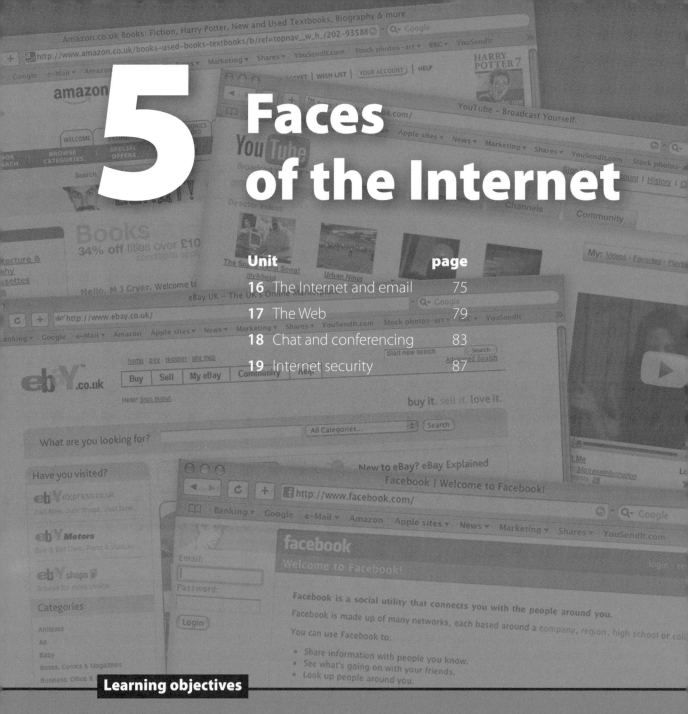

5 Faces of the Internet

Learning objectives

In this module, you will:

- study vocabulary related to the Internet and email.
- learn how to form different types of question.
- learn about the basic features of the Web.
- learn and use collocations related to the Internet.
- learn and use vocabulary related to the Web, e-commerce, online banking, online chatting and videoconferencing.
- learn and use abbreviations in online chats.
- learn about the basic ideas related to security and privacy on the Internet.
- discuss controversial issues related to the Internet.

The Internet and email

Topics

Getting online
Internet features
Email

Learning objectives

To acquire vocabulary related to the Internet and email
To understand how the Internet works
To understand the anatomy of an email
To be able to form different types of question correctly

Language

Grammar: Questions
Vocabulary: *modem, Internet Service Provider (ISP), wireless router, online, TCP/IP, broadband, ADSL, Wi-Fi, wireless access point, hotspot, power-line Internet*

Internet features: *email, FTP (file transfer protocol), newsgroups, Telnet, chat and instant messaging*
Email features: *mail server, email client, username, @, domain name, attachment, emoticon, smiley, spam*

Skills

Listening: Completing notes based on a conversation in a computer shop
Speaking: Asking and answering questions about the Internet
Reading: Understanding general and specific information from a selection of FAQs about the Internet
Writing: Writing a reply to an email

Plan

Teacher's activities	Students' activities	Comments
Module page You may want to point out the learning objectives for your SS.	SS familiarize themselves with the topics and objectives of the Module.	
1 Internet basics **A** Encourage SS to give a good definition of the Internet. Write the best on the board. Point out the use of the article in **the** *Internet*. Contrast with SS' mother tongue if necessary. **B** Elicit SS' ideas and write them on the board. **C** Play track 20 of the CD and ask SS the question: *Why do you think the sales assistant has to explain so much about the Internet?* **D** Play the CD again, pausing if necessary. Draw SS' attention to the difference between the *Internet* and the *Web*.	**A** SS discuss how they would define *the Internet*. **B** SS make a list of the things they can use the Internet for. **C** SS listen to the conversation and answer the question. **D** SS listen and complete the notes.	Web browsers include *Internet Explorer*, *Mozilla Firefox* (free, open-source), *Safari*, *Netscape*, and *Opera* in order of descending popularity (2006). PDAs and mobiles use micro-browsers (e.g. *Opera Mobile*). You may like to give SS a copy of the audio script. In *Infotech*, *Internet* is written with a capital *I* when we are referring to *the Internet*. In other cases – for example, *internet café* or *internet use* – it is written with a lower-case *i*. The same applies to *the Web*. Other variations exist, but point out to SS that they should be consistent in their writing.

2 Internet FAQs **A and B** Check that SS understand what FAQs are. Monitor the tasks, helping with any vocabulary problems (especially terms like *TCP/IP, broadband* and *hotspot*). **C** Ask SS to read Part 2 of the article again and find the words that match the definitions.	**A** SS read Part 1 and choose the correct answers. **B** SS decide which internet system they would use to do the tasks. SS then read Part 2 and check their answers. **C** SS find the corresponding words.	FAQ stands for *Frequently Asked Question*. It is a common feature of many websites. Make sure SS can distinguish features like *FTP, Telnet* and *newsgroups*.
3 Language work: questions **A and B** Refer SS to the HELP box, providing more examples if necessary. Monitor the tasks, helping where needed.	**A** SS make a question about Sue Clarke for each of her answers. **B** SS make questions using prompts and practise asking and answering them.	We don't use an auxiliary verb when the subject is the interrogative pronoun, e.g. *Who* sent this email? *What* happened? *Wh-* questions generally have falling intonation in English, but not in some other languages (e.g. Spanish).
4 Email **A** Write an email address on the board and explain the format. Draw SS' attention to the email message and its parts. Ensure SS understand terms like *username, @ (at), domain name, attachment* and *spam*. **B** You may like to set this task for homework.	**A** SS find the basic features of email in the text and the illustration. **B** SS write a reply to the email message.	**POP3** (Post Office Protocol) **email accounts** are handled by programs like Outlook Express or Eudora; when you check your mail, all new messages are downloaded to your own computer. **Web-based email** is accessible from websites like Hotmail or Gmail.

Evaluation of the unit:

Answer key

1 Internet basics

A

Possible answer

The Internet, or Net, is a global network of computer networks, which allows organizations and individuals to share all sorts of information and computer resources.

B

Possible answers

You can send and receive email, explore the Web, transfer files, have live conversations, take part in online forums, use remote computers. You can use the Web to find and download games, music or videos, buy products online, search for information, etc.

C

Possible answer

The woman doesn't seem to know much about the Internet, or computers in general.

D

1 computer
2 modem
3 Internet Service Provider (ISP)
4 wireless
5 radio
6 email, file transfer, newsgroups, real-time chats, instant messaging, looking for information on the Web
7 pages

2 Internet FAQs

A

1c   2a   3c   4c   5b   6b

B

1b   2f   3e   4c   5a   6d

C

1 mailing list
2 web browser
3 log into
4 message thread
5 newsreader

3 Language work: questions

A

Possible answers

1 How old are you?
2 What do you do? / What's your job?
3 What do you do in your job? / What does your job involve?
4 How long have you been doing this job?
5 When did you graduate from university?

B

1 What type of internet connection do you have at home?
2 How fast is your internet connection?
3 How much do you pay for broadband access?
4 How often do you access the Internet?
5 Which email program do you use?
6 Who do you send email to?
7 Do you use a mobile phone to access the Internet?
8 Do you use the Internet in public spaces using Wi-Fi?
9 Do you play games online?
10 How many newsgroups do you subscribe to?

4 Email

A

1 mail server
2 email client / mail program
3 username
4 Subject
5 attachment
6 emoticons or smileys
7 spam

B

Open task

Audio script

Assistant: …so that's £549 including VAT. Is there anything else I can help you with?

Customer: Well, would you mind explaining how I access the Internet with this computer? I don't think I really even understand what the Internet is! Wait a minute, I'm going to write this down.

Assistant: Of course. Well, basically, the Internet is a global network of computer networks, which allows users to share all kinds of information and computer resources. The system is made up of networks interconnected all over the world, from universities and large corporations to commercial online systems and non-profit organizations …

Customer: OK, that sounds complicated enough! And can I access the Internet automatically with this PC?

Assistant: Well, you need a computer and a modem – a device that connects your PC to the telephone line. You'll also need an account with an Internet Service Provider, or ISP – that's a company that offers connection to the Internet for a monthly fee.

Customer: OK, that sounds easy, but what if we have several computers in different rooms. How can I connect them all to the Internet?

Assistant: In that case, the best choice is a wireless router with a built-in modem. It's a device that links various computers over a network and will connect everyone in your family to the Internet without using cables.

New computers include wireless support but if any of the computers are old, you'll need a Wi-Fi wireless adapter.

Customer: I'm sorry, but what does Wi-Fi mean exactly?

Assistant: Wi-Fi is short for *Wireless Fidelity* and refers to a technology that uses radio waves to communicate data over medium range distances.

Customer: Right. And so that's everything?

Assistant: Not quite. You'll need some software too, specifically internet connection software and a Web browser application, such as Internet Explorer or Mozilla Firefox.

Customer: OK, I think I've got it. And I'll be able to start emailing straight away?

Assistant: You can do more than just email. There's file transfer, newsgroups, real-time chats, instant messaging and looking for information on the Web.

Customer: Wow, this all sounds complicated. I'm not sure I even understand the difference between *the Web* and *the Internet*.

Assistant: Well, the Web is a huge collection of 'pages' stored on computers all over the world. Web pages contain all sorts of information in the form of text, pictures, sounds and video. The Internet is the network which connects all the computers.

Customer: OK, I think I've got it.

Topics
A typical web page
Web phenomena
E-commerce and online banking

Learning objectives
To recognize the basic features of the Web
To use collocations related to the Web and the Internet
To acquire vocabulary related to the Web, e-commerce and online banking

Language
Collocations
The prefixes *e-* and *cyber-*
Vocabulary: *website, hyperlink, search engine, download, upload, blog, podcast, peer-to-peer, wikis, e-tailer, RSS feed, shopping cart, internet auction, phishing*
Parts of a Web address

Skills
Listening: Recognizing the pronunciation of internet addresses
Understanding general and specific information about e-commerce and online banking from a podcast, and taking notes
Speaking: Discussing web-surfing habits
Reading: Understanding general and specific information from a text about web phenomena
Writing: Writing a short article about present and future web phenomena

Optional materials
Web pages illustrating different web phenomena, e.g. eBay, Wikipedia, MySpace, YouTube, Second Life, Facebook, etc.

Plan

Teacher's activities	Students' activities	Comments
1 A typical web page **A** Draw SS' attention to the screenshot and encourage them to identify the basic features of a web page. **B** Monitor the task, helping with any vocabulary problems. **C** Play track 21 of the CD. Make sure SS can correctly pronounce and recognize @, *dot* (.) and *slash* (/).	**A** SS look at the screenshot of a typical web page and try to say the features in English. **B** SS read the text and label the features on the screen with the terms in bold. **C** SS listen to the pronunciation of some internet addresses and write them down.	Make sure SS learn how to say the format of a web address in English. For extra practice, ask SS to read aloud different email and web addresses.
2 The collectives of cyberspace **A, B** and **C** Monitor the tasks, helping with any vocabulary problems. **D** Encourage SS to write about websites they think are important or will be important in the future. You may like to set this task for homework.	**A** SS read the text and choose appropriate websites to carry out particular tasks. **B** SS read the text again and match the sentence beginnings to the correct endings. **C** SS find words in the text with the appropriate meanings. **D** SS write a short article for a newsletter about the latest web phenomena.	The reading passage is a tour of web phenomena and shows the power of peer-to-peer software and user-generated content (e.g. wikis, blogs and podcasts).

3 Language work: collocations 2

A Refer SS to the HELP box, providing more examples if necessary. Encourage SS to recognize and learn collocations, as they will help them to speak and write English in a more natural and accurate way.

B and **C**
Monitor the tasks, helping where needed.

A SS match the words on the left with the words on the right to make collocations.

B SS make sentences using the collocations.

C SS find the collocations in the sentences and say what type they are.

In Unit 1, we focused on verb-noun collocations. This language work focuses on the other types of collocation that exist in English. Make sure SS don't confuse a *collocation* (two words that often appear together) with a *compound* (two words used as a single word, e.g. *hard drive*).

4 E-commerce and online banking

A Play track 22 of the CD and ask SS the question: *What is each speaker talking about?*

B You may like to pre-teach the terms *shopping cart*, *PIN*, *TAN* (transaction authorization number) and *phishing*.
Play the CD again.

C Monitor the task, helping where needed. Do not give the answers for Task C yet, as SS will listen for them in Task D.

D Play the CD a third time for SS to check their answers to **C**.

A SS listen to an extract from a monthly podcast and identify what each speaker is taking about.

B SS listen again and make notes under the headings.

C SS complete the gaps with words from the box.

D They listen again and check their answers.

You may like to give SS a copy of the audio script.

5 Language work: the prefixes *e-* and *cyber-*

A Refer SS to the HELP box, providing more examples if necessary (*e-shopping, e-calling, cyberworld, cybermen, cyberphobia, cyberattack, cybercast, cyborg* – a part robot, part human organism)

B Encourage SS to use an online dictionary to help them. If you do not have access to the Internet in class, you may like to set this task for homework.

A SS complete the definitions with words from the HELP box.

B Using the Internet, SS find the meaning of *e-* words.

The *e-* prefix is often added to activities that have moved from the physical world to its 'electronic' alternative.

6 What do you use the Web for?

Monitor the discussions, helping where needed.

SS discuss the questions with a partner.

Evaluation of the unit:

80

Answer key

1 A typical web page

A

Open task

B

a go back one page	g search box
b go forward one page	h feed button
c URL address	i clickable hypertext link
d go to the home page	j clickable image link
e refresh the current page	k show favourites
f stop the current transfer	

C

1 http://www.cambridge.org/elt
2 ftp://ftp.ftpplanet.com
3 http://www.britannica.com/heritage

2 The collectives of cyberspace

A

1 Google	5 Flickr
2 Amazon	6 eBay
3 MoveOn	7 BitTorrent
4 YouTube	

B

1e   2c   3a   4b   5d

C

1 wikis	3 videoblog	5 podcast
2 e-tailer	4 Skype	

D

Open task

3 Language work: collocations 2

A

1 a and e	4 b
2 b and c	5 f
3 a and b	6 d

B

Possible answers

- Online encyclopedias are easier to search than traditional ones.
- Sites like MoveOn are encouraging more people to take action when they feel strongly about something.
- I'm not allowed to use my work email for personal use so I use Hotmail to email friends.
- As soon as I get back from holiday I upload my photos to Flikr.
- I need to get a portable player to listen to music on the way to work.
- Before I see a film, I go to the official website to find out more about it.

C

1 be online (verb + adv); browse the Web (verb + noun); visit chat rooms (verb + noun); send and receive emails (verb + noun)
2 Instant messaging (adjective + noun); great way (adjective + noun); communicate with (verb + particle)
3 fully compatible (adverb + adjective)
4 plug into (verb + particle)
5 highly addictive (adverb + adjective); addictive game (adjective + noun)
6 virtual reality (adjective + noun)

4 E-commerce and online banking

A

Speaker one: e-commerce
Speaker two: online banking

B

Possible answers

Speaker 1
Things people buy online
- Books, music and airline tickets
Steps for buying online
- Enter a site dedicated to e-commerce and browse their products
- Put the items you want to buy into a virtual shopping cart
- Enter your personal data – you may have to log in with a username and a password if you have an account with them
- Confirm the order and log out
Precautions
- Read all product information clearly
- Check whether you can cancel the purchase
- Keep a printout of your order
- Do not give private information that is not directly required for your transaction
- Only give your credit card number to suppliers that you know and trust
- Make sure the website is secure

Speaker 2

Things you can do with online banking
- Access an account, check balances, pay bills, transfer funds at any time to anywhere

Biggest issue with online banking
- Security and cybercrime

Precautions
- Never give your PIN to anyone and don't even write it down
- Be careful of *phishing*
- Don't provide any sensitive information
- Don't forget to have anti-spy software

C

1 internet auction
2 browse
3 shopping cart
4 log in
5 authorization
6 fake; steal

D

Students listen again and check their answers to C.

5 Language work: the prefixes *e-* and *cyber-*

1 cyberslacker
2 e-card
3 e-zine
4 cybercafé
5 cybercrime
6 e-voting
7 e-signature
8 e-assessment
9 e-cash
10 e-book

6 What do you use the Web for?

Open task

Audio script

Extract 1

Like many people, I regularly buy things online, mostly books, music and airline tickets. Many online retailers offer good rates or discounts. Occasionally, I also buy things on internet auction sites such as eBay, where people sell things to the highest bidder.

There are four main steps to buying online. First, you enter a site dedicated to e-commerce and browse their products. Then you put the items you want to buy into a virtual shopping cart, a program that lets you select the products and buy with a credit card. Thirdly, you enter your personal data – you may have to log in with a username and a password if you have an account with the site – and finally, you confirm the order and log out.

But before buying things online, you should take a few basic precautions. Read all the product information clearly; check whether you are entitled to cancel the purchase; always keep a printout of your order; don't give any private information that is not directly required for your transaction, for example about your shopping habits; only give your credit card number to suppliers that you know and trust, and make sure their website is secure.

Extract 2

Online banking is the term used for performing transactions and payments through a bank's website. The greatest advantage of online banking is obviously convenience. I can access my account, check balances, pay bills and transfer funds at any time and to anywhere.

But the big issue with online banking is of course security and cybercrime. Most banks use various layers of authentication to prevent fraud: they give you a PIN with a username and a password, and for some transactions you'll be required to use a TAN, a transaction authorization number.

Nevertheless, there are some basic precautions you should take.

Never give your PIN to anyone and don't even write it down. Be aware of *phishing* – you may receive fake emails claiming to be from your bank and asking for personal information or account details in an attempt to steal your identity. Don't provide any sensitive information unless you're sure it's your bank that is requesting it. Finally, don't forget to invest in some good anti-spy software.

Chat and conferencing

Topics
Online chats and instant messaging
Videoconferencing
Internet telephony
Cybercafés
Netiquette

Learning objectives
To acquire specific vocabulary related to online chatting and videoconferencing
To use abbreviations in online chats

Language
Chat abbreviations: ASAP, BBS, BFN, BTW, F2F, GL, H&K, IC, ILU, IMO, IOW, LOL, TIA, UR, 2, 4, B, C, R, U

Vocabulary: *chat room, Instant Messaging, videoconference, internet telephony, buddy list, virtual reality, avatar, nickname, cybercafé, netiquette, FAQ, flame war, spamming*

Skills
Listening: Deciding if information from an interview is true or false
Speaking: Discussing chatting habits
Planning a cybercafé
Reading: Matching headings to paragraphs in a text
Finding specific information from a text
Writing: Participating in an imaginary chat session, using abbreviations
Making plans for your own cybercafé

Plan

Teacher's activities	Students' activities	Comments
1 Online chatting Encourage SS to talk about their own experiences. With younger SS, pay special attention to Question 3: *Do you give out personal details in chat rooms? Why should you be careful about it?*	SS discuss the questions.	This unit has linguistic and professional value – i.e. how to set up and behave in online meetings.
2 Virtual meetings **A**, **B** and **C** Monitor the tasks, helping with any vocabulary problems. In Task A, encourage SS to read the text quickly. They will be reading it in more detail in Task B.	**A** SS match the headings to the correct paragraphs. **B** SS read the passage again and find answers to the questions. **C** SS find the words in the text.	Make sure SS distinguish between *chat rooms* and *Instant Messaging*. Refer them to the Glossary if necessary.
3 Netiquette **A** Tell SS that there are certain netiquette (net etiquette) rules that we should follow if we want to use online chatting and forums correctly. **B** Monitor the discussions, helping where needed.	**A** SS take the netiquette quiz. They may like to read more about this topic on the Web. **B** In pairs, SS talk about their experiences of bad netiquette.	You may need to explain the terms *FAQ, flame war* and *spamming*. Use a dictionary if necessary.

4 R u free 4 a chat?

A SS may know many of these abbreviations already so set the task before referring SS to the HELP box to check their answers.
Encourage SS to find more abbreviations on the Web.

B Tell SS to rewrite the dialogue using abbreviations.
You may like to ask SS to act out the dialogue.

C Read through the task with SS and make sure they understand it properly.
Monitor the chats, helping where needed.

D Monitor the discussions, helping where needed.

A SS write the full forms of the abbreviations used in an IM chat. SS then look at the HELP box to check their answers.

B SS rewrite an IM chat using abbreviations.

C In pairs, SS practise having an online conversation. They write short notes to each other, using abbreviations where possible.

D In pairs, SS discuss questions about their chatting habits.

Some people think that IM is destroying the ability of young people to make coherent texts, but this is not true. It is a question of register. For example, the language used in an essay or a job interview is different from the language used in a casual conversation or SMS; they simply belong to different registers. You may like to explain this to your SS.

5 At a cybercafé

A Elicit answers from SS.

B Play track 23 of the CD and ask the question: *Does Daniel like where he works?*

C Play the CD again, pausing if necessary.

A SS discuss the questions.

B SS listen to an interview with the manager of a cybercafé and answer the question.

C SS listen again and do the true/false exercise.

6 Plan your own cybercafé

A Monitor the task, helping where needed. Encourage SS to be creative.
You may like to set this task for homework.

B Encourage SS to present their plan to the class, using PowerPoint if possible.

A In small groups, SS plan how they would open a cybercafé in their town.

B A spokesperson from each group presents the plan to the class.

This task is like a mini-project that combines writing and speaking.

Evaluation of the unit:

Answer key

1 Online chatting

Open task

2 Virtual meetings

A

a4   b1   c3   d5   e2

B

1 It enables virtual workgroups to communicate easily over long distances; they can exchange ideas and information as if they were in the same room.
2 A webcam and a conferencing program, for example Netmeeting or CU-SeeMe.
3 Internet telephony, also known as VoIP
4 Web chat rooms allow multiple users to join in a conversation and see what all the other people are typing; they are based around certain themes (love, music, business, etc.). Instant Messaging, however, refers to chatting privately with a select person or group of people, usually with friends or colleagues.
5 With a username and password.

C

1 flat-rate
2 Instant Messaging / IM
3 buddy list (buddy = friend)
4 in real time
5 virtual reality
6 avatars

3 Netiquette

A

1 True
2 you're shouting
3 Giving out personal or financial information
4 posting unsolicited advertising messages.
5 read the FAQs (Frequently Asked Questions)
6 angry responses or offensive comments
7 True

B

Open task

4 R U free 4 a chat?

A

Abby: By the way, where are you going for your holiday?
Sue: Girona. Have you been?
Abby: Yes. I went to Girona last summer.
Sue: Did you have a good time?
Abby: It's great, in my opinion. How are you going to travel?
Sue: We're flying.
Abby: Where are you staying?
Sue: In a youth hostel.
Abby: I see. In other words, the cheapest place possible!
Sue: Laughing out loud! Yes. By the way, any recommendations?
Abby: Let me think. I'll send you a message as soon as possible.
Sue: Thanks in advance.
Abby: Got to go. Bye for now!

B

Paulo: BTW, r u free on Saturday?
Emma: Sure – it would b good 2 meet F2F. Shall we go 4 a coffee?
Paulo: Good plan. Café Moka makes the best coffee, IMO.
Emma: It's the closest 2 ur house IOW!
Paulo: LOL! Yes, ur right! But the coffee really is good.
Emma: C u at 4?
Paulo: Great. BFN.

C and D

Open tasks

5 At a cybercafé

A

Open task

Possible answers for 2

Web browsing, email, chat rooms, Instant Messaging, internet telephony, games, a word processor, fax and printing services, magazines, and the services of a traditional café (tea, coffee, etc.)

B

Yes, he says it's the kind of place he'd like to spend time even if he didn't work there.

C

1 True
2 True
3 False – They **do** help people if they have problems. **For beginners, they give a tutorial**.
4 False – One week is **£18**.
5 True
6 False – You **don't** have to pay long-distance phone rates on the Internet.
7 True

6 Plan your own cybercafé

Open task

Audio script

Journalist: Daniel, how would you describe Cyberstop?

Daniel: It's essentially a place where you can use computers to access the Internet. Once you're online, it's up to you what you do. There's a range of services that we'll allow people to use, from browsing the Web and multiplayer gaming to internet telephony.

Journalist: And what about people who need some help with using all this?

Daniel: Not a problem. We always try and be available to help people if they've got problems. For beginners, we like to give a tutorial to get them going.

Journalist: And how much do you charge for using the computers?

Daniel: What most people do is come in and use our machines for a fee. We usually charge two pounds an hour. But some customers prefer to have unmetered access, so we give them a pass for a day or a week. One day costs four pounds, one week is eighteen pounds. That can't be bad!

Journalist: And what sort of people tend to come to the Cyberstop?

Daniel: Many customers are travellers or students who want to access webmail and Instant Messaging services to keep in touch with family and friends. We've got huge numbers of Latin American users, we've got Americans, Greeks, Russians. We pretty much cover the globe at the moment. However, we don't tend to get that many English users, probably because they've got access at home. But we are able to provide communication services to people who would otherwise have to make long-distance telephone calls. And we can be considerably cheaper than just picking up the phone and dialling.

Journalist: Is it possible to offer all this technology and still have the friendly atmosphere of a traditional café?

Daniel: I think we try to. It's the kind of place I'd like to spend time, even if I didn't work here! We've had to separate out the computers from the café a little bit, so upstairs is the café area where you can sit and drink coffee and play chess and cards or sit and chat to people …

Topics

Security and privacy on the Internet
Safety online for children
The history of hacking
Computer crimes

Learning objectives

To understand the basic ideas related to security and privacy on the Internet
To discuss controversial issues related to the Internet

Language

Grammar: The past simple
Vocabulary: Internet security: *username, password, firewall, hacker, cracker, cookies, worm, Trojans, spyware, adware, digital certificate, encryption, decryption, filtering program*
Internet crime: *piracy, plagiarism, malware spreading, phishing, cyberstalking, IP spoofing*

Skills

Listening: Choosing the best answers to questions about an interview
Completing the interviewer's notes
Speaking: Discussing internet issues: computer crimes, personal privacy, infringement of copyright, censorship, etc.
Reading: Understanding general and specific information about security and privacy on the Internet
Finding specific information in a text about the history of hacking
Writing: Summarizing a discussion (on PowerPoint, if possible)

Plan

Teacher's activities	Students' activities	Comments
1 On alert **A** Elicit answers from SS. **B** Direct SS' attention to the pictures and ask them to do the matching exercise. If necessary, explain the key words: *https_ (secure), padlock, password, spyware* and *firewall*.	**A** SS discuss the questions. **B** SS match the captions with the pictures.	The Internet offers a lot of benefits, but there are risks as well. Make sure SS understand that no computer system is completely safe.
2 Security and privacy on the Internet **A** Monitor the task, helping with any vocabulary problems. **B** and **C** Monitor the tasks, helping with any vocabulary problems and reviewing technical terms connected with the Internet if necessary.	**A** SS scan the article to see how many of their ideas from 1A are mentioned. **B** SS read the text in more detail and answer the questions. **C** SS solve the clues and complete the puzzle.	*Hackers*: the good guys who hack code (write software); *crackers:* the bad guys who break security on computer systems. Most people use the term *hacker* for both.

3 Safety online for children

A Play track 24 of the CD, pausing if necessary.

B Play the CD twice more. You could extend the activity by asking SS the questions: *Do you agree with the member of the Internet Safety Foundation about the risks of the Net? Should websites rate their content?*

A SS listen and choose the best answers according to the interview.

B SS listen again and complete the interviewer's notes.

You may like to encourage SS to find examples of web-filtering software on the Internet to see how it works.

4 The history of hacking

A Monitor the task, helping with any vocabulary problems.

B Monitor the discussions, helping where needed.

A SS read Part 1 of the text to find answers to the questions.

B SS discuss the cases in Part 1.

5 Language work: the past simple

A Refer SS to the HELP box, providing more examples if necessary. Refer SS to the list of irregular verbs on page 166.

B Ask SS to prepare at least five questions about the landmarks in internet history. Stronger SS could prepare more than five.

C Monitor the task, checking that SS are using the past simple correctly.

A SS read Part 2 of the text and complete it with the correct past form of the verbs.

B SS read some landmarks in the history of the Internet and prepare some questions in the past simple.

C In pairs, SS ask and answer their questions.

Encourage SS to surf the Web and find out more about the history of the Internet.

6 Internet issues

A Read through the list of crimes on the Internet and encourage SS to discuss the questions in small groups. Suggest that each group nominates one person to take notes to help them in Task B.

B Monitor the task, helping where needed. Encourage SS to use PowerPoint to present their summary.

A SS discuss the questions in groups.

B SS then write a summary of the discussion. Finally, a spokesperson for each group presents their views to the rest of the class.

Online task

Visit www.cambridge.org/elt/ict for an online task related to the topic of this module.

Evaluation of the unit:

Answer key

1 On alert

A

Possible answers

1 A hacker is someone who obtains illegal or unauthorized access to computer data.
2 It's difficult, but it's definitely possible to break into computer systems and read confidential information.
3 You can protect your computer by using anti-virus software and a personal firewall. You shouldn't open emails from strangers.

B

1d   2c   3a   4b

2 Security and privacy on the Internet

A

Hacker used to be the general word for a person who was interested in computers. *Cracker* was the word used to describe someone who used their computer skills to break into people's computers for criminal gain. Now the word *hacker* is used to mean *cracker*. In the computer business, hackers who use their skills for good are known as *white hats* while crackers are known as *black hats*.

B

1 Because the Internet is an open system and we are exposed to hackers and crackers who break into computer systems to steal or destroy data. Security is vital when we send sensitive information or credit card numbers.
2 Mozilla Firefox displays a lock when the website is secure and it warns you if the connection is not secure; it also allows you to disable or delete cookies.
3 Banks use SSL (Secure Sockets Layer), a protocol which provides secure transactions.
4 We can encode our email using an encryption program like Pretty Good Privacy.
5 The most common methods to protect private networks (intranets) are passwords for access control, firewalls, and encryption and decryption systems.
6 A virus can enter a PC via an infected disc or via the Internet.
7 A worm spreads through email attachments; it replicates itself and sends a copy to everyone in an email address book.

C

	1	p	a	s	s	w	o	r	d		
	2	f	i	r	e	w	a	l	l		
		3	h	a	c	k	e	r			
		4	v	i	r	u	s	e	s		
5	f	r	e	e	w	a	r	e			
6	e	n	c	r	y	p	t	i	o	n	
7	d	e	c	r	y	p	t	i	o	n	
		8	s	p	y	w	a	r	e		

3 Safety online for children

A

1a   2a   3b

B

1 privacy	4 aimed
2 offensive	5 filtering
3 propaganda	6 rate

4 The history of hacking

A

1 Kevin Mitnick hacking into the North American Defense Command in Colorado Springs
2 1981
3 He was arrested in connection with virus spreading after the Union Bank of Switzerland almost lost £32 million to hackers.
4 15

B

Open task

5 Language work: the past simple

A

1 was	6 overwrote
2 showed	7 infected
3 attempted	8 stole
4 launched	9 weren't affected
5 spread	

B and C

Open tasks

6 Internet issues

Open task

Audio script

Journalist: The Internet is a great resource for kids, but some parents are concerned about the presence of 'indecent' material. Can the Internet be dangerous for children?

Diana Wilson: Well, the Net obviously brings a lot of benefits for education and entertainment, but it's not always a friendly place. We've all heard of things like the manipulation of children, invasions of privacy, distribution of indecent or offensive material, violence, and racist propaganda.

Journalist: And what sort of precautions should parents take?

Diana Wilson: It's impossible for parents to be with their children at every moment. But there are plenty of websites aimed at children, and some programs can help parents control information. But this is no substitute for education. It's the parents' role to make their children aware of both the benefits and the risks of the Internet.

Journalist: And what else can parents do? I mean, are there any technological solutions?

Diana Wilson: Yes, web software companies have developed filtering programs that let parents block objectionable websites and restrict access to specific aspects of the Net. Some organizations have also proposed that websites should rate their content with a label, from child-friendly to over-18 only. Other people argue that internet ratings aren't good, because they limit free expression on the Net.

Journalist: That's obviously a very controversial topic. What about internet addiction? What can parents do if their children spend too much time online?

Diana Wilson: Well, if they're obsessed with games or spend so much time online that their lives are affected negatively, parents should establish a balance between internet use and other activities. When there are strong signs of internet addiction, they should consider seeking professional help.

6 Creative software

Learning objectives

In this module, you will:

- learn and use vocabulary related to graphics software.
- learn how to describe graphics.
- study the basic features and vocabulary related to desktop publishing.
- discuss the pros and cons of e-publishing versus paper publishing.
- write a letter to a newspaper.
- learn about the main components and applications of multimedia systems.
- learn how to use conditional sentences.
- study the basic principles of web page design.
- learn how to use common modal verbs.
- design a mock home page for a college or company.

Unit 20 | Graphics and design

Topics

2-D and 3-D graphics

Graphics software: tools and functions

Learning objectives

To acquire vocabulary related to graphics software

To identify the function of different graphics tools

To discuss the applications of computer graphics

To describe graphics

Language

Grammar: The *-ing* form

Uses of the gerund

Vocabulary: Graphics: *raster graphics (bitmaps), vector graphics, resolution, jagged, filters, composite, CAD, wireframe, solid modelling, rendering, fractals, GIS*

Toolbox: *marquee select tools, move tool, crop, paintbrush, eraser, paint bucket, eyedropper, zoom, colour palette*

Skills

Listening: Listening for general and specific information in an online tutorial

Speaking: Discussing the benefits of using computer graphics

Choosing appropriate graphics software for particular tasks

Reading: Finding general and specific information from a text about computer graphics

Writing: Describing graphics

Optional materials

The toolbox of a graphics program (e.g. Windows Paint or Adobe Photoshop)

Plan

Teacher's activities	Students' activities	Comments
Module page You may want to point out the learning objectives for your SS.	SS familiarize themselves with the topics and objectives of the Module.	
1 Computer graphics **A** Refer SS to the pictures and elicit answers to the questions. Do not give the answers for Questions 3 and 4 yet, as SS will read for them in Task B. **B** You may want to pre-teach some vocabulary (*2-D and 3-D images, drawing program, CAD – computer aided design*) to prepare SS for the reading passage. **C** Monitor the task, helping with any vocabulary problems. Encourage SS to guess the meaning of new words from context. **D** Make sure SS have understood these basic terms: *resolution, filter, wireframe, rendering* and *fractal* **E** Monitor the discussions, helping where needed. Ask SS to justify their answers.	**A** SS look at the pictures and answer the questions. **B** SS read the text and check answers to Questions 3 and 4. **C** SS read the text again and answer the questions. **D** SS match the terms to the correct definitions. **E** In pairs, SS discuss which application of computer graphics they think is the most important or useful.	2-D drawings have no depth or perspective – they look flat; 3-D pictures do have depth. SS should be able to distinguish between *raster graphics* (bitmaps) and *vector graphics*.

2 Language work: the *-ing* form
  A and **B**
    Refer SS to the HELP box, providing more examples if necessary. Monitor the tasks, helping where needed.

A SS read the sentences, identify the *-ing* forms and decide if they are a gerund, a present participle or an adjective.
B SS correct the mistakes in the sentences.

The infinitive is studied in Unit 24.

3 The toolbox
  A You may like to personalize this task by asking SS: *Have you ever used a graphics package with these or similar tools? Do you know how to use the toolbox of programs like Photoshop, Freehand, or Windows Paint?*
  Play track 25 of the CD, pausing if necessary.
  B Play the CD twice more if necessary.
  C Monitor the task, helping where needed.

A SS listen to an extract from an online tutorial and answer the questions.
B SS listen again and complete the extract.
C SS match the graphics tools with the correct functions.

Each graphics package has its own painting and drawing tools.

Task B is a good opportunity to practise the use of the gerund.

4 Choosing graphics software
  Refer SS to the *Useful language* box and back to the text on page 101. Monitor the discussions, helping where needed. Ask SS to justify their answers.

SS work in pairs. Student A chooses a task from the list and describes it; Student B chooses the most appropriate graphics software for that task. SS then swap roles.

5 Describing graphics
  Draw the SS' attention to the pictures showing the stages involved in drawing a plane using graphics software and refer them to the *Useful language* box and the text on page 101.
  You may like to set this task as homework.

SS write a short description under each picture.

Evaluation of the unit:

Answer key

1 Computer graphics

A

1 a and d are three-dimensional; b and c are two-dimensional.

2 3-D images represent objects (like the car here) more accurately; in graphs, they can also illustrate different quantities more clearly.

3 **Possible answers**

   a Businesspeople

   b Architects

   c Cartographers (map makers)

   d Car engineers or designers

4 **Possible answers**

   Designers in all kinds of industries to design and test products; engineers (e.g. telephone and electrical engineers) to plan circuits; weather forecasters to show changes in weather; economists to illustrate economic development; web designers to create pages for the Web; scientists in research; journalists in broadcasting; teachers; students.

B

SS check their answers to 3 and 4.

C

1 Raster graphics represent images as bitmaps. This means they are stored as pixels, which can become jagged or distorted when manipulated. Vector graphics, however, represent images as mathematical formulas, so they can be changed or scaled without losing quality.

2 JPEG, GIF, TIFF and EPS

3 Compositing is assembling multiple images to make a single final image

4 Computer Aided Design

5 Computer graphics can be used to develop, model and test car designs before the physical parts are made; this can save money and time.

6 GIS (Geographic Information Systems)

7 Computer animation is used by animators to create cartoons or to add effects in movies and video games.

D

1e   2d   3a   4f   5b   6c

E

Open task

2 Language work: the -ing form

A

1 g (after a preposition)   4 pp (present continuous)

2 a   5 g (complement of a verb)

3 g (after a preposition)   6 pp (reduced relative clause)

B

1 Computer animation is the process **of creating** objects which move across the screen.

2 *Texturing* involves **adding** paint, colour and filters to drawings and designs.

3 You can open the colour palette **by clicking** on the corresponding icon.

4 CAD programs are very fast **at performing** drawing functions.

5 A lot of time and money is saved **by testing** a car design **before making** the product.

6 **Rendering** refers to the techniques used to make realistic images.

3 The toolbox

A

1 A toolbox is a collection of drawing and painting tools that enable you to manipulate images in graphics software.

2 Primitives are the basic shapes used to make graphical objects. They are usually geometric, for example lines, circles, etc.

3 Attributes are the colour, line type, fill area, interior style, etc. of each primitive.

4 Translation means moving an object to a different location.

B

1 painting   6 drawing

2 select   7 rotating

3 make   8 turning

4 clicking   9 Scaling

5 draw

C

1b   2j   3a   4i   5g   6c   7h   8e   9f   10d

4 Choosing graphics software

Possible answers

1f   2e   3c   4d   5a   6b

5 Describing graphics

Possible answers

2 In this second stage, the designer has used *solid modelling*, which creates a three-dimensional representation of the solid parts of the object; now the aeroplane looks solid, with volume.

3 The third stage is called *texturing the model*, which means adding paint and colour to the different areas. The designer has used dark blue and yellow.

4 Finally, the design is *rendered* to make the plane look realistic. Rendering techniques include shading, light sources and reflections. The sky background adds realism to the picture. As a finishing touch, the designer might use animation to make the plane move.

Audio script

Graphics programs usually have a toolbox – a collection of drawing and painting tools that enable you to type, select, draw, paint, edit, move and view images on the computer.

The basic shapes which are used to make graphical objects are called primitives. These are usually geometric, such as lines between two points, arcs, circles, polygons, ellipses and even text. Furthermore, you can specify the attributes of each primitive, such as its colour, line type, fill area, interior style and so on.

The various tools in a toolbox usually appear together as pop-up icons in a menu or palette. To use one, you activate it by clicking on it. For example, if you want to draw a rectangle, you activate the rectangle tool, and the pop-up options give you the possibility of drawing rectangles with square or rounded corners.

You can transform an object by translating, rotating, or scaling it. *Translation* means moving an object to a different location. *Rotation* is turning the object around an axis. For example, you may need to rotate an object 90 or 180 degrees to fit the drawing. *Scaling* is making the object larger or smaller. Now, if you need …

Topics

Desktop publishing (DTP)
Steps in a DTP publication
e-publishing versus paper publishing

Learning objectives

To understand the basic features and vocabulary related to desktop publishing

To discuss the pros and cons of e-publishing versus paper publishing

To write a letter to a newspaper asking for information about the hardware and software used in its production

Language

Grammar: order of adjectives

Vocabulary: *DTP, page layout, font, kerning, text flow, master pages, toolbox, PDF file, service bureau, Computer-To-Plate (CTP), platesetter*

Skills

Listening: Identifying the correct order of steps in the production of a DTP publication from an online tutorial

Speaking: Discussing the pros and cons of e-publishing versus paper publishing

Reading: Checking and finding specific information in a text about desktop publishing

Writing: Writing a formal letter requesting information

Optional material

A page-layout program like *Adobe InDesign* or *QuarkXPress*

Plan

Teacher's activities	Students' activities	Comments
1 What is desktop publishing? **A** Monitor the discussions, noting any vocabulary problems that arise. Do not give the answers for Task A yet, as SS will read for it in Task B. **B, C** and **D** Monitor the tasks, helping where needed. **E** Encourage SS to do the task with their books closed.	**A** SS discuss the questions. **B** SS read the article to check their answers to **A**. **C** SS read the text again and find answers to the questions. **D** SS find the terms corresponding to the definitions. **E** SS try to answer the question: *What is desktop publishing?*	This unit is particularly useful for graphic arts students. You may like to show SS a page-layout program such as *QuarkXPress* or *Adobe InDesign*. Make sure SS understand these key concepts: *DTP, page layout, PDF, Computer-To-Plate (CTP)* and *platesetter*

2 Language work: order of adjectives

A Refer SS to the HELP box, providing more examples if necessary. You may want to write the usual order of modifiers before the headword on the board (opinion, description, origin, material, purpose + headword).

B Encourage a contrastive analysis of adjective order in English and SS' mother tongue. If you do not speak your SS' mother tongue, ask them to correct each other's work.

C Monitor the task, helping where needed.

A SS rewrite the descriptions in the correct order.

B SS translate the sentences and then explain how modifiers are placed in their own language.

C In pairs, SS describe an object in their classroom or office.

Make sure SS understand that adjectives of opinion (subjective) come before adjectives of description (objective).

There may occasionally be exceptions to the usual order of adjectives.

3 Steps in a DTP publication

A Monitor the task, helping with any vocabulary problems. Do not give the answer for Task A yet, as SS will listen for it in Task B.

B Play track 26 of the CD.

C Draw SS' attention to the illustration and help with any vocabulary problems. SS may like to translate the terms into their mother tongue.

A SS put the steps in the creation of a DTP document into the correct order.

B SS listen to an online tutorial and check their answers.

C SS label the features of a page designed with *Adobe InDesign*.

You may like to give SS a copy of the audio script.

4 Writing a letter

A Read the rubric with the SS. It is important that SS recognize that letters are still regularly used in formal correspondence. Ask SS the question: *What is the writer asking for?*

B Draw SS' attention to the structure and features of a formal letter.

C Encourage SS to use the phrases presented in **B** in their own letter. You may like to set this task for homework.

A SS read the model letter and find the purpose of writing.

B SS match different features of the letter with the correct descriptions.

C SS write a letter to a newspaper asking for information about the hardware and software used in its production.

Point out that *We would be very grateful if you could …* and *Could you also tell us …* are examples of rather formal requests, often used in letters of this kind.

5 e-publishing versus paper publishing

A Read the short web extract with the SS and list the examples of e-publishing mentioned. Elicit more examples if possible.

B Monitor the task, helping where needed. If you need to feed ideas to the teams, see the list of pros and cons in the answer key.

C Encourage SS to use connectors of opinion and contrast.

A SS look at a web extract and find examples of e-publishing.

B SS work in teams. Team A prepares a list of the advantages of paper publishing over e-publishing; Team B prepares a list of the advantages of e-publishing over paper publishing.

C SS debate their ideas and decide which team has the most convincing position.

Let SS use the Web to find arguments for their discussion.

You may like to organize a vote on this issue: *Will e-publishing replace printed books?*

Evaluation of the unit:

Answer key

1 What is desktop publishing?

A

1 **Possible answers:** Books, newspapers, magazines, newsletters, leaflets, brochures, posters, advertisements and business cards.
2 **Possible answers:** Text, charts and graphs, drawings and illustrations, and photographs

B

SS check their answers to A.

C

1 A page-layout program (also called a *desktop publishing program* or DTP program)
2 DTP software is different from a word processor in that it uses high-quality scalable fonts and gives you control over typographic features such as kerning. Another difference is the text flow feature.
3 PDF means Portable Document Format, a standard format developed by Adobe which allows people to view, search and print documents exactly as the publisher intended.
4 Adobe Acrobat Reader
5 Because CTP machines are expensive, and service bureaux offer services such as scanning and printing.

D

1 font
2 kerning
3 text flow
4 printing plate
5 platesetter

E

Open task

2 Language work: order of adjectives

A

1 user-friendly desktop publishing software
2 a reliable, young hardware company
3 the German graphic design industry
4 modern word processing applications
5 a new Sony portable music player

B and C

Open tasks

3 Steps in a DTP publication

A

1a   2c   3e   4d   5f   6b

B

SS check their answers to A.

C

1 dimensions
2 horizontal ruler
3 toolbox
4 guide
5 scanned photo
6 layout of master pages

4 Writing a letter

A

The writer is asking for information about the kind of DTP software that the newspaper uses and wants to find out how long the paper's online edition has been running for.

B

1b   2a   3e   4c   5d   6f   7g   8h

C

Open task

5 e-publishing versus paper publishing

A

Online newspapers and magazines, blogs, e-books

B and C

Open tasks

Possible ideas

e-publishing	Paper
Advantages	
Cheaper to publish	Robust and durable
Can be downloaded instantly	Requires no power source
Easier to update	Comfort and pleasure of reading print media
Takes up little space	Nice look, feel and smell
Environmentally friendly (no dead trees)	Buying and lending books and sharing newspapers/magazines is fun
Disadvantages	
Can be incompatible with hardware/software	Can be expensive to produce
Devices like e-book readers can be stolen/damaged	Cannot be easily copied/shared
	Take up space
Not a great format for visual artwork, large maps, etc.	Can weigh a lot and be difficult to move
Batteries can run out	

Audio script

… so let's begin. First, the DTP designer decides the basic form of the document (the type of document, general design, colour, fonts, images required, etc.).

To create the DTP document, the designer begins by selecting a template or by specifying the settings of a new document (the page size, margins, columns, paragraph styles, master pages, etc.).

The next step is to type the text directly or to import it from a word processing program like Word or WordPerfect.

When the text has been edited, the designer imports the pictures and uses precise tools to position, scale, crop and rotate all the items.

Once the file is composed and saved, the designer has to prepare it for printing, which involves verifying the colour specification, creating a Postscript or PDF file, exporting the file in HTML format for the Web, checking proofs, etc.

The last step is to take the files to a service bureau, which will print the publication.

Topic
Multimedia technologies and applications

Learning objectives
To understand the main components and applications of multimedia systems
To acquire specific vocabulary related to multimedia software
To use conditional sentences correctly

Language
Grammar: First and second conditional sentences
Vocabulary: *multimedia, hypertext, hypermedia, interactivity, sound card, MIDI, digital audio*

workstation (DAW), electronic encyclopedia, streaming, webcast, CD ripper, plug-in, animation, video computing, video editing

Skills
Listening: Completing a diagram with information from a conversation in a computer shop
Speaking: Discussing the applications of multimedia
Reading: Matching headings to paragraphs in a text about multimedia
Finding specific information in a text and correcting technical mistakes
Writing: Writing a post for a blog, summarizing the present and future of multimedia

Plan

Teacher's activities	Students' activities	Comments
1 Multiple forms of media Elicit from SS the different types of content that can be integrated into multimedia applications, and the different products that incorporate multimedia. Write SS' suggestions on the board.	SS discuss the questions.	*Multimedia* = multiple forms of media
2 Components and system requirements **A** Play track 27 of the CD, pausing if necessary. **B** You may like to draw the diagram on the board. Play the CD again.	**A** SS listen and choose the correct answers. **B** SS listen again and complete the diagram of a multimedia system.	SS should be able to distinguish between hardware components and software sources.
3 Multimedia magic! **A** Encourage SS to read the text quickly. They will be reading it in more detail in Task B. **B** Tell SS to find evidence for their answers in the text. **C** You may need to explain some of the vocabulary in more depth. Refer SS to the Glossary if necessary.	**A** SS match the headings with the correct paragraphs. **B** SS read the text again and correct the technical mistakes in the sentences. **C** SS match some key words with the definitions.	Make sure SS learn key terms like *hypertext, hypermedia, MIDI, DAW, streaming, webcast, CD ripper* and *video editing*

4 Language work: conditional sentences **A** Refer SS to the HELP box, providing more examples if necessary. Monitor the task, helping where needed. **B** Monitor the discussions, checking that SS are using the second conditional correctly.	**A** SS read the HELP box and complete the sentences with the correct form of the word in brackets. **B** SS discuss *what they would do if they …*	The study of conditional clauses (type 1 and 2) is contextualized by using examples from the reading text. You may like to present them on the board. For weaker SS, a contrastive analysis of conditional clauses with their own language may be helpful.
5 Applications of multimedia **A** Draw the SS' attention to the pictures and help with any vocabulary problems. **B** Refer SS to the *Useful language* box. Monitor the discussions, helping where needed. **C** You may like to set this task for homework.	**A** SS match the descriptions with the pictures. **B** In pairs, SS discuss how multimedia is used in five situations. SS then present their ideas to the class. **C** SS write a post for a blog, summarizing what multimedia is, what it can do, and their predictions for the future.	Encourage SS to use the Web to find more information about the applications presented in **A**.

Evaluation of the unit:

Answer key

1 Multiple forms of media

Possible answers

1 Multimedia applications can combine text, high-quality sound, graphics, photo images, animation and full-motion video.
2 E-books, encyclopedias and dictionaries (on CD-ROMs or DVDs), slide presentations, computer games, web pages, movies, 3G mobile phones, virtual reality systems, information kiosks, computer-based training courses.

2 Components and system requirements

A

1b   2b   3a

B

1 Fast
2 High-quality
3 Sound

4 speakers
5 headphones
6 Microphone
7 interactive
8 animation
9 rippers

3 Multimedia magic!

A

a4   b1   c3   d2

B

1 Multimedia training software is distributed on **optical discs (and over the Internet)**.
2 You need to have **a sound card** on your computer to hear speech and music.
3 **MIDI** allows your computer to communicate with electronic musical instruments.
4 A CD ripper converts CDs to **MP3 format**.
5 The Encyclopedia Britannica is available **in print, online, on DVD, and as a concise version for iPods, PDAs and mobile phones.**

C

1b   2e   3c   4d   5a

4 Language work: conditional sentences

A

1 bring
2 don't have
3 had
4 'd buy
5 'd invest

B

Open task

5 Applications of multimedia

A

a4   b3   c5   d1   e2

B

Possible answers

Touch screen information kiosks: free information (maps, photos); applications in libraries, hotels, museums, airports, etc.

A business presentation: use of PowerPoint (integrate all forms of media; position text, graphics, movies and transitions on slides)

MMS mobile phones: multimedia messaging service (send and receive text, images, audio, video clips); can include weather reports, news, sport bulletins, etc.

Virtual reality: use multimedia content (3-D graphics, sounds); apply VR in video games, virtual exhibitions, medical surgeries, flight and engineering simulations, etc.

Distance learning: interactive CDs/DVDs; use of multimedia in delivery systems (email, videoconferencing); online lessons, etc.

C

Open task

Audio script

Customer: What exactly is *multimedia*? This encyclopedia says it's the *multimedia version*.

Assistant: Well, multimedia refers to technologies and applications that integrate different types of media – so, things like text, sound, video, computer graphics, animation, that kind of thing.

Customer: And what's so good about it, then?

Assistant: Well, it can make things more interesting and entertaining to use. Good examples are the Encyclopedia Britannica and Encarta, which present information in more exciting ways than traditional encyclopedias. For instance, you can look up information about the Second World War in a print encyclopedia, but if you use the multimedia version, you can look at maps, listen to speeches, watch video clips, or click hyperlinks that take you to other screens. The experience is more engaging, and you probably even learn more quickly. Another good example is interactive games, which, when they're combined with virtual reality techniques, let you interact with a simulated world full of 3-D graphics and sounds.

Customer: OK, well I'm not really interested in games, but the encyclopedia sounds like the kind of thing my family would use. What do I need to run it?

Assistant: First off, you'll need a computer with a fast processor and a lot of RAM. You'll also need a high-quality monitor, a large hard drive and a DVD drive.

Customer: I suppose you also need some sort of sound capability?

Assistant: Yes, of course. Modern computers come with a sound card and stereo speakers or headphones. If you want to record audio, you'll need a decent microphone.

Customer: Right. And what about special software?

Assistant: Yes, access to sound and video requires Windows Media Player or Apple QuickTime. Access to interactive media requires a program like Adobe Flash. Some multimedia software also includes video and audio editing software, animation software, hypermedia databases, CD and DVD rippers …

Photocopiable © Cambridge University Press 2008

Web design

Topic

Website and blog design

Learning objectives

To understand the basic principles of web page design

To acquire vocabulary related to web design

To use modal verbs correctly

To design a mock home page for a college or company

Language

Grammar: Modal verbs

Vocabulary: *website, web page, home page, blog, HTML tag, web editor, cascading style sheets (CSS), body text, background, frames, hyperlink, RSS feed, plug-in, Java applet*

File formats: *.wav, .ra, .mp3, .avi, .mov, .mpg*

Skills

Listening: Putting the steps in the design of a website into the correct order based on information from an interview

Deciding whether certain web design guidelines are right or wrong based on information from an interview

Speaking: Discussing questions about website design

Describing a personal website

Discussing a blog you would like to write

Reading: Finding specific information in a text about web page design

Writing: Designing a mock home page for your college or company

Writing a blog entry

Optional material

A web editor

Samples of home pages from favourite websites or blogs

Plan

Teacher's activities	Students' activities	Comments
1 A typical home page Draw SS' attention to the *Yahoo!* home page and monitor the discussions, noting any vocabulary problems that arise. If any SS have a blog or personal website, encourage them to describe it.	SS look at a typical home page and answer the questions. If any student has a blog or site of their own, they describe its homepage.	Make sure SS know the difference between a *website* and a *web page* (see Answer key). SS should also be able to distinguish between a *personal website* and a *blog*.
2 Web page design **A** and **B** Monitor the tasks, helping with any vocabulary problems. Draw SS' attention to the web page displayed and to some basic HTML tags.	**A** SS read the text and find the specific information. **B** SS match the sentence beginnings with the correct endings.	Some SS may like to learn a few basic HTML tags. They can view the source HTML code of any page by choosing the *Page Source* option in the View menu of their browser. Make sure SS learn these basic terms: *HTML, web editor, tags, cascading style sheet, frame, hyperlink, Java applet* and *RSS feed*.

3 Language work: modal verbs

A SS should try to find the modal verbs in the text before looking at the HELP box.

B Refer SS to the HELP box, providing more examples if necessary.

C Monitor the discussions, checking that SS are using the modal verbs correctly.

A SS find all of the modal verbs in the text.

B SS study the form and semantics of modal verbs and then complete the sentences with suitable modal verbs.

C In pairs, SS discuss the five questions, using appropriate modal verbs.

A note on *needn't*:

i) You needn't do it. (modal)
ii) You don't need to do it.
iii) You don't have to do it.

ii and iii above are equivalent to i, but do not behave as modal verbs. Some people say that all three forms are in fact modal verbs, which is incorrect from a linguistic point of view.

4 Designing a website

A Ask SS to discuss the questions in pairs. You may like to write a summary of their answers on the board.

B Tell SS they are going to listen to an interview with an expert describing the most important steps and guidelines in web design. Play track 28 of the CD.

C Play the CD again, pausing if necessary.

D If SS have access to a web editor, encourage them to use it. If not, then have SS draw their designs or mock up the page in Word.
You may like to set this task as homework.

A SS give examples of favourite websites and discuss what makes a good site.

B SS listen to the interview and put the steps in the correct order.

C SS tick (√) the good design principles and cross (X) the bad ones.

D SS design a homepage for their college/company.

You may like to give SS a copy of the audio script.

D is like a mini-project. Help SS organize the contents.

5 Blogs

A Elicit answers from SS. Refer SS to the Glossary for the definition of *blog* if necessary.

B Write the differences between a blog and a personal website on the board.

C Monitor the discussions, helping where needed.

D Monitor the task, helping where needed. You may like to set this task as homework.

Online task

Visit www.cambridge.org/elt/ict for an online task related to the topic of this module.

A In pairs, SS try to define what a blog is and say which blogs they visit regularly.

B SS look at a screenshot and list some design differences between a blog and a normal website.

C SS ask their partners questions to find out the features of the blog they'd like to write.

D SS write an entry for the blog they have described in **C**.

In 1997, Jorn Barger coined the term *web log* for an online diary, and this soon became *blog*. As a verb, *to blog* means to maintain or add content to a blog. Some people say there is a difference between a website and a blog: a website is often the location of a web-based business; a blog, however, is an online diary or journal where a blogger can write personal comments about a particular topic. But note that a lot of websites include blogs, and a blog is a form of website, so the distinction is becoming blurred.

Remind your SS of other words made up from *blog*: *to blog, blogger, video blog (vlog), blogosphere, news blog*, etc.

Evaluation of the unit:

Answer key

1 A typical home page

Possible answers

1

Companies have websites in order to promote projects and advertise products. In some cases, the website *is* the company's business. For example, there are portals that provide a full range of web services including email, e-commerce, forums, news, entertainment, etc. Specialist portals are related to particular subjects, such as music or sports. Portals that provide links to other websites on a particular topic are also called supersites. They can include news and information about the subject as well as personal comments.

2

A website is a collection of web pages (usually including a home page), set up by an organization or an individual, which are usually stored on the same server. A website contains many web pages. A website is like a book, and web pages are the pages of the book. The pages are all linked together; you can move from one page to another by clicking on words or pictures called hyperlinks. Some websites have a site map that shows the layout of the entire site.

A web page is an individual document on the Web, identified by its own unique URL. Web pages contain different elements, such as text, pictures, video, links, etc.

3

A home page is the introductory page that tells visitors what information is contained on a website. It has links to the other areas of the site. It can also include information such as when the site was built or updated. A home page is also the default start-up page on which a web browser starts.

4

Open task

2 Web page design

A

1 HTML (hypertext markup language)
2 web editor (e.g. Macromedia Dreamweaver, Microsoft FrontPage)
3 .pdf (the portable document format)
4 frames

5 .jpg (joint photographic experts group), .gif (graphics interchange format), and .png (portable network graphics)
6 .avi (audio video interleave), .mov (QuickTime movie) and .mpg (moving picture experts group)

B

1c   2e   3a   4b   5d   6f

3 Language work: modal verbs

A

The following modals appear in the text: *needn't, can, could, should, may, must. Might* is referred to in the HELP box but doesn't appear in the text. Other modal verbs include *will* (see Unit 30) and *would* (see Unit 22).

B

1 can/could
2 can/could
3 needn't
4 should
5 must
6 may/might
7 Can/Could/May

C

Open task

4 Designing a website

A

Open task

B

1 Decide the content and structure for the website
2 Write and format the text
3 Insert computer graphics and sounds
4 Link related pages to each other using hyperlinks
5 Publish the website
6 Keep the website updated

C

1 Right
2 Right
3 Wrong
4 Wrong
5 Wrong
6 Wrong
7 Right
8 Right

D

Open task

5 Blogs

A

Possible answer

1

A blog is a user-generated website where people express their opinions. The entries are displayed in reverse chronological order.

2

Open task

B

Possible answer

Blogs tend to be more text-heavy than websites; entries are listed chronologically (in reverse order); blogs tend to user fewer graphics; they make use of embedded video; they have a lot of links, normally posted within the blog entries themselves; they don't often have home pages.

C

Open task

D

Open task

Audio script

Interviewer: Sarah, what's the first step in building a website?

Sarah: First of all, you should always plan it carefully. Decide what sort of information you're going to include and how you're going to organize it. I like to start with the home page, because this is the starting point of your site, almost like the table of contents in a book. It's a good idea to design the site on paper first – a few diagrams will help you clarify the relationships between the pages.

Interviewer: That sounds sensible. What editing tool do you recommend?

Sarah: I recommend using a web editor; it'll make it easier to design your site. You can download a web editor from the Internet quite easily.

Interviewer: I suppose a big part of the job is writing the text and formatting the pages.

Sarah: Yes. You need to type the text and decide the formatting effects. You can also apply styles to text and other page elements.

Interviewer: And what about graphics and sounds?

Sarah: Well, that's the next step. You can insert all sorts of pictures and sounds, but they should have a clear purpose, some sort of communicative intention. Don't insert photos or animations just to make the pages look nice, and avoid having a large number of graphics.

Interviewer: Why's that?

Sarah: Because graphics can take a long time to download, and visitors might give up and leave.

Interviewer: I see. Any advice about the use of colour?

Sarah: It's fun to experiment with colour. You may like to choose different colours for the background and the text. But make sure that all the text is easy to read and avoid very bright colours.

Interviewer: OK. What's next?

Sarah: Once you've created and saved a few pages, it's time to join them together with hyperlinks. A good design principle is not to put too many links on one page – people may lose patience or get distracted. And check that all the links work, since web addresses sometimes change.

Interviewer: So, be careful with links. What do I do if I then want to publish my website on the Net?

Sarah: To publish your site, you have to find a web server and then transfer all the files from your PC to the server. This is called *going live*.

Interviewer: Right, sounds easy! Any final comments, Sarah, before we take some calls?

Sarah: Yes, try to keep the pages updated, improving the content and design if necessary. And the final touch: always include the date to show that your site is up-to-date.

7 Programming / Jobs in ICT

Learning objectives

In this module, you will:

- study basic concepts in programming.
- learn and use vocabulary connected with programming and become familiar with word families.
- ask and answer questions about computer languages.
- learn and use the basic vocabulary associated with the Java language.
- talk about your personal experience of using computers.
- practise the use and pronounciation of the -ed form of verbs.
- discuss the personal qualities and professional skills needed for a job in ICT.
- learn how to understand job advertisements.
- learn how to write a CV and a letter applying for a job.

Program design and computer languages

Topics
Steps in programming
Computer languages

Learning objectives
To understand basic concepts in programming
To acquire vocabulary connected with programming and to become familiar with word families
To ask and answer questions about computer languages
To use the infinitive correctly

Language
Grammar: The infinitive
Vocabulary: Programming: *flowchart, coding, machine code, bug, debugger, debugging, source code, object code, low-level language, high-level language,* *assembler, compiler, interpreter, object-oriented programming, programmer, markup language, markup tag*
Computer languages: *FORTRAN, COBOL, Pascal, BASIC, Visual BASIC, C, C++, Java, HTML, XML, VoiceXML*

Skills
Listening: Putting the steps of a process in order based on information from a training course
Speaking: Asking and answering questions to complete a table of information about two programming languages
Reading: Finding specific and general information in a text about computer languages
Writing: A short explanation of how a program is written, based on notes

Plan

Teacher's activities	Students' activities	Comments
Module page You may want to point out the learning objectives for your SS.	SS familiarize themselves with the topics and objectives of the Module.	
1 Programming **A** and **B** Direct SS' attention to the *C* program. Elicit answers from SS and write the best definitions on the board. Compare them with the definition provided in the Glossary.	**A** SS brainstorm their ideas about what programming is. **B** SS compare their definition of programming with the one provided in the Glossary.	The illustration shows a simple *C* program.
2 Steps in programming **A** Monitor the task, helping where needed. Practise the pronunciation of the terms. Do not give the answer for Task A yet, as SS will listen for it in Task B. **B** Play track 29 of the CD for SS to check their answers. **C** Play the CD again, pausing if necessary. Alternatively, you may like to ask SS to say *stop* or raise a hand after each programming step. **D** Play the CD a third time and ask SS to take notes. Monitor the task, helping where needed.	**A** SS match the technical terms with the definitions. **B** SS listen to a software developer talking to some SS about how a program is written and check their answers to **A**. **C** SS listen again and put the programming steps into the correct order. **D** SS listen again, take notes and write a short explanation of each step in their own words.	

3 Computer languages

A Encourage SS to read the text quickly to find the answers. They will be reading it in more detail in Task B.

Write the computer languages on the board.

B Ask SS to provide evidence from the text for their answers.

If SS are having trouble grasping the basic concepts, draw their attention to the diagram on p121.

C Monitor the task, helping where needed.

A SS read the text quickly and say how many high-level languages are mentioned.

B SS read the text again to find answers to the questions.

C SS complete the sentences with a computer language from the text.

Make sure that SS understand these basic concepts: *machine code, low-level language, high-level language, compiler, interpreter* and *markup language*. Refer SS to the Glossary if necessary.

4 Word building

Remind SS that they can expand their vocabulary by becoming familiar with word families. You may like to remind SS of other adjectival and nominal suffixes.

SS decide what part of speech the words are and complete the sentences with the correct form.

5 Language work: the infinitive

A and **B**

Refer SS to the HELP box, providing more examples if necessary.

C Monitor the discussions, checking that SS are using the infinitives correctly.

A SS make sentences using the prompts.

B SS choose the correct words to complete the sentences.

C In pairs, SS discuss questions that involve the use of infinitive.

Remind SS that other verbs are followed by the *-ing* form, not by the infinitive (see Unit 20).

6 Visual BASIC and VoiceXML

A Encourage SS to cover the text that their partner is working from with a piece of paper.

B Monitor the task, helping where needed.

A and **B**

SS work in pairs. Student A reads about Visual BASIC and completes his/her table only. Student B reads about VoiceXML and completes his/her table only. SS then ask their partner about the other language to complete the table.

Evaluation of the unit:

Answer key

1 Programming

A

Open task

B

SS compare their answer to A with the Glossary.

2 Steps in programming

A

1c   2a   3d   4e   5b

B

SS check their answers to A.

C

1 Understand the problem and plan a solution
2 Make a flowchart of the program
3 Write instructions in a programming language
4 Compile the program (to turn it into machine code)
5 Test and debug the program
6 Prepare documentation

D

Open task

3 Computer languages

A

Eight: FORTRAN, COBOL , BASIC, Visual BASIC, PASCAL, C, C++, Java

B

1 No, computers don't understand human languages because the processor operates only on machine code.
2 An assembler is a special program which converts a program written in a low-level language into machine code.
3 To make programs easier to write and to overcome the problem of intercommunication between different types of computer.
4 PASCAL
5 A compiler translates the source code into object code (machine code) in one go. However, an interpreter translates the source code line by line, as the program is running.

6 Because they use instructions called markup tags to format and link text files.

C

1 XML
2 FORTRAN
3 Java
4 VoiceXML
5 COBOL

4 Word building

> program (n or v)
> programmers (n)
> programming (n or present participle of v)
> programmable (adj)

1 programming
2 program
3 programmers
4 programmable

> compile (v)
> compiler (n)
> compilation (n)

5 compilation
6 compiler
7 compile

> bug (n or v)
> debug (v)
> debugger (n)
> debugging (n or present participle of v)

8 bug
9 debugger; debug
10 debugging

5 Language work: the infinitive

A

2 It's expensive to set up a data-processing area.
3 It's advisable to test the programs under different conditions.
4 It's unusual to write a program that works correctly the first time it's tested.
5 It's important to use a good debugger to fix errors.
6 It's easy to learn Visual BASIC.

B

1c   2b   3b   4c   5c   6a   7a   8b

C

Open task

6 Visual BASIC and VoiceXML

A

	Visual BASIC	VoiceXML
What does Visual BASIC / Voice XML stand for?	Beginner's All-purpose Symbolic Instruction Code	Voice EXtensible Markup Language
When was it developed?	1990 (by Microsoft)	2000
What are its main features?	Instead of writing a lot of instructions to describe interface elements, the programmer adds pre-defined objects, such as buttons, icons, etc.	For input, it uses voice recognition; for output, it uses pre-recorded audio content and text-to-speech.
What is it used for?	To create Windows applications	To make Web content accessible via the telephone. Voice applications: web portals, intranets, e-commerce, home appliances.

B

Open task

Audio script

I'd like to begin the course by giving you a very basic overview of the programming process. We'll then move on to the details. So, to write a program, we normally follow these steps:

A program usually provides a solution to a given problem – for example, how to calculate wages and income tax in a big company. First of all, you have to understand exactly what the problem is and define it clearly. This means you have to decide, in a general way, how to solve the problem. The next step is to design a step-by-step plan of instructions. This usually takes the form of a flowchart, a diagram that uses special symbols to show how the computer works through the program – where it makes decisions, where it starts and ends, where data is input, things like that.

Next, you write the instructions in a programming language, like BASIC, Pascal or C. These computer instructions are called source code. Then you have to use a compiler, a special program that converts the source code into machine code – the only language understood by the processor, which consists of 1s and 0s.

Once you've written the program, you have to test it with sample data to see if there are any bugs or errors. The process of correcting these errors is called debugging. Computer programmers have to find the origin of each error, write the correct instruction, compile the program again, and test it until it works correctly.

Finally, you have to write program documentation, a detailed description of how to use the program. A great program is not much good unless people know how to use it.

Photocopiable © Cambridge University Press 2008

Topics

The Java language

Your own computer history

Learning objectives

To acquire the basic vocabulary associated with the Java language

To talk about your personal experience of using computers

To practise the use and pronunciation of the -ed form of verbs

Language

Grammar: The use and pronunciation of the -ed form (in the past simple, past participle and adjectives)

Vocabulary: *Java applet, plug-in, platform independent, object-oriented, bytecode, multi-threaded, source code, compiler, interpreter*

Skills

Listening: Checking answers to a gap-fill exercise based on information from a lecture

Speaking: Asking and answering questions about your personal experience of using computers

Reading: Correcting true/false statements about the basic features of Java based on information from a text

Writing: Making notes about your experience of using computers

Plan

Teacher's activities	Students' activities	Comments
1 Java applets **A** To introduce the topic, you may like to elicit answers to the questions: *What is Java? What are Java applets?* Draw SS' attention to the pictures illustrating Java applets. Monitor the task, noting any vocabulary problems that arise. **B** Monitor the activity, helping where needed.	**A** SS match the examples of Java applets to the correct descriptions. **B** SS match the terms with the definitions.	Some SS may have heard or used the Java language before.
2 The Java language **A** Monitor the task, helping with any vocabulary problems. Ask SS to provide evidence from the text to support their answers. **B** Remind SS that these are examples of collocations (word partners) and encourage SS to learn them. **C** SS may need to look back at the text to help them.	**A** SS read the statements and the text and make changes to the false statements. **B** SS match each word on the left with its partner to make a common technical term. **C** SS complete the sentences with the correct -ed form in the box.	Some SS may have heard or used the alternatives to Java: Microsoft's C# and Adobe Flash. Encourage SS to say something about them, perhaps comparing them to Java. Task C introduces the topic of the language work in **3**.

3 Language work: the -ed form

A This task is designed to help SS recognize and practise the pronunciation of the -ed form. Refer SS to the HELP box before they carry out the task.

B Read the infinitives out loud for SS to check their answers.

C This passage includes more background information about Java and recycles regular and irregular verb forms. Do not give the answers for Task C yet, as SS will listen for them in Task D.

D Play track 30 of the CD, twice if necessary, for SS to check their answers.

A and **B**
SS put the -ed forms into the correct columns and then listen to check their answers.

C SS complete the extract about Java with the correct form of the verbs in the box.

D They then listen to the lecture and check their answers.

SS may have trouble deciding whether a verb form is pronounced /t/ or /d/. SS may also over-use the /ɪd/ ending. Make sure SS pronounce /ɪd/ only after the sounds /t/ and /d/.

4 Your experience with computers

A Monitor the task, helping where needed.

B Refer SS to the *Useful language* box. Monitor the discussions, checking that SS are using past tenses correctly.
Choose a few SS to tell the class briefly about their partners. Ask a few questions to get an idea of your SS' average computer history.

A SS make notes about the different stages in their own computer history.

B SS share their experiences with another student.

This task is a good opportunity for SS to practise the use of the past simple (see Unit 19).

Evaluation of the unit:

Answer key

1 Java applets

A

a4   b1   c3   d5   e2

B

1c   2e   3a   4b   5d

2 The Java language

A

1 Java was invented by **Sun Microsystems**.
2 With the **compiler**, a program is first converted into Java bytecodes.
3 Java **is** compatible with most computing platforms.
4 The Java language is **multi-threaded**, **various parts** executing at the same time.
5 Java **does** have competitors: Microsoft's C# and Adobe Flash.
6 Flash files are called **flash movies.**

B

1a 2d 3f 4b 5c 6e

C

1 animated
2 object-oriented
3 compiled; interpreted
4 used
5 configured
6 pronounced

3 Language work: the -ed form

A

/t/	/d/	/ɪd/
stopped	described	decided
asked	called	executed
produced	programmed	object-oriented
watched	configured	persuaded
published	arranged	converted
	designed	

B

1   decided
2   developed
3   called
4   had
5   based
6   renamed
7   could
8   were
9   began
10 supported

C

SS listen and check their answers to C.

4 Your experience with computers

Open task

Audio script

… is now used in millions of web pages. The idea for Java started in 1990, when a team of software engineers at Sun Microsystems decided to create a language for a handheld device that could control and interact with various kinds of electronic appliances, ranging from Nintendo Game Boys to VCRs and TV set-top boxes. They developed an object-oriented programming language that one of the engineers, James Gosling, called *Oak*, after the tree outside his window. The device even had an animated character named *Duke*, who would go on to become Java's mascot.

With the advent of the Web in 1993, the company made a web browser based on the Oak language. Later on, this language was adapted to the Internet and renamed *Java*. The 1.0 version of Java was officially introduced by Sun in May 1995.

At that time, web pages could only display text, pictures and hyperlinks. With the arrival of Java, web designers were able to include animation and interactive programs on web pages. The first major application created with Java was the HotJava browser. The Java language began to attract serious attention from the internet community and was soon supported by Netscape Navigator and MS Internet Explorer. Today, Java is a hot technology that runs on multiple platforms, including smart cards, embedded devices, mobile phones and computers.

Topics
Jobs in ICT
Job advertisements
Job application letter
Curriculum vitae

Learning objectives
To discuss the personal qualities and professional skills needed for a job in ICT
To understand job adverts
To write a CV in English and a letter applying for a job

Language
Grammar: The present perfect
Vocabulary: *software engineer, hardware engineer, blog administrator, help desk technician, DTP operator, network administrator, webmaster, computer security specialist*
Professional skills

Skills
Listening: Identifying ICT jobs from speakers' descriptions
Completing notes about a candidate, based on a job interview
Speaking: Discussing qualities and abilities required for particular jobs
Reading: Identifying the qualities and skills required for jobs from written adverts
Finding specific information in a job application letter
Writing: A CV and a job application letter

Plan

Teacher's activities	Students' activities	Comments
1 IT professionals **A** Monitor the task, helping where needed. You may like to ask SS to brainstorm more jobs in ICT. **B** Play track 31 of the CD, pausing if necessary.	**A** SS complete the sentences with the jobs from the box. **B** SS listen to four people speaking and identify the jobs.	Some other jobs in ICT: database analyst, systems analyst, database administrator, computer operator, computer trainer, technical writer, IT consultant, internet researcher, online teacher, computer animator
2 Job advertisements **A** Monitor the task, helping with any vocabulary problems. You may like to explain the abbreviations CV (curriculum vitae) and DTP (desktop publishing). **B** Ask individual SS if they would be interested in any of the jobs. Ask SS to justify their answers. **C** Monitor the task, helping with any vocabulary problems.	**A** SS read the adverts and, in pairs, decide which qualities and abilities are most important for the jobs. **B** SS discuss the question. **C** SS look at the profile of Charles Graham, choose the most suitable job for him, and give reasons.	

3 A letter of application

A Introduce the letter by explaining that it was written by an applicant for one of the jobs advertised in Task 2.

B Refer SS to the HELP box, providing more examples if necessary.

A SS read the letter and answer the questions about it.

B SS complete the letter with *for, since, ago* or *until*.

4 A job interview

Play track 32 of the CD, pausing if necessary. You may like to ask SS the questions: *Did Sarah answer the questions well? Would you give her the job?*

SS listen to the job interview and complete the notes.

You may like to give SS a copy of the audio script.

5 Language work: the present perfect

A Refer SS to the HELP box, emphasizing the difference between the present perfect simple and continuous.

B Refer SS back to the HELP box, making sure they understand the contrast between the present perfect and past simple. Provide more examples if necessary.

C Monitor the discussions, checking that SS are using the tenses correctly.

A SS read the HELP box and then choose the correct tense to complete the sentences.

B SS put the verbs into the present perfect simple or past simple.

C SS make questions using the prompts. SS then ask and answer the questions.

A contrastive analysis with SS' mother tongue may help them to understand the differences.

6 Applying for a job

A Read through the advert with SS and help them relate María Quintana's CV (at the back of the book) to the job. Remind them of the layout of a formal letter (see Unit 21).

B and C
Encourage SS to write their own CVs. You may like to set these tasks for homework.

A SS read the advert and identify what the company is looking for. SS then decide what aspects of María Quintana's CV are relevant for the job and write a letter of application. SS can use the letter in Task 3 as a model.

B SS write their own CV.

C SS think of the job of their dreams and write a letter of application for it.

Make sure SS are using the present perfect and past simple tenses correctly.

In addition to the sample CV in the book, SS can search on the Web for advice on writing a CV in English.

Online task

Visit www.cambridge.org/elt/ict for an online task related to the topic of this module.

Evaluation of the unit:

Answer key

1 IT professionals

A

1 hardware engineer	5 network administrator
2 software engineer	6 webmaster
3 blog administrator	7 computer security specialist
4 DTP operator	8 help desk technician

B

Speaker 1: webmaster
Speaker 2: help desk technician
Speaker 3: hardware engineer
Speaker 4: computer security specialist

2 Job advertisements

A

Open task

Some other qualities or abilities which could be added to the list: enthusiasm, good communication skills, reliability, punctuality, versatility, confidence, ability to work under pressure, ability to cope with routine work.

B

Open task

C

Charles Graham's experience and qualifications mean he is more suited to the DTP operator position.

3 A letter of application

A

1 Senior Programmer
2 She saw the advertisement in *The Times*.
3 She has been working as a software engineer for (the last) three years.
4 She has written programs in COBOL (for commercial use) and in C (for large retail chains).
5 She spent three months in Spain two years ago.

B

1 until   2 For   3 since   4 ago

4 A job interview

1 Computer Sciences
2 Analyst programmer for a year
3 general commercial use
4 IBM mainframes
5 Microsoft Access and dBase 5
6 wants something more demanding and with more responsibility; wants to learn about a new industry

5 Language work: the present perfect

A

1 's never liked	4 have you written
2 've been working	5 's been writing
3 's been using	6 've interviewed

B

1 's been	4 've lost
2 worked	5 sent
3 Have you ever worked	

C

1 Have you ever lived or worked in another country?
2 Have you ever had a bad job interview?
3 Have you ever done a job you hated?
4 How long have you been studying English?
5 How long have you been using computers?
6 How many emails have you received today?
7 How many jobs have you applied for this year?

6 Applying for a job

A

Possible answer

James Taylor
eJupiter Computers
37 Oak Street
London SW10 6XY
3rd May 2008

Dear Mr Taylor,

I am writing to apply for the position of Webmaster, which was advertised on monster.com on April 21st.

I graduated in 2004 with a degree in Computer Science and Engineering from the University of Madrid. After I left university, I did a course in computer hardware and networking at the Cybernetics College, London. In 2005 I completed a course in web design, where I learnt to use HTML, Java and Macromedia Dreamweaver. I also have a diploma in web-based technology for business.

For the last three years I have worked part-time at keo.es, where I have been responsible for updating the website regularly. I have also been using Adobe Flash to create media animation. Before taking my present job, I worked as an IT consultant at Media Market, a company specializing in e-commerce and IT strategies.

I studied languages at school and have the Cambridge CAE certificate in English. When I was a teenager I spent several years in Morocco so I also have a fluent level of Arabic. I have knowledge of most computer platforms (Windows, Mac and Linux) and good communication skills. In my spare time I like listening to music and travelling.

I now feel ready to take the next step in my career and would welcome the opportunity to work for a company like eJupiter. I enclose my curriculum vitae and I look forward to hearing from you. I will be available for an interview at any time from Monday.

Yours sincerely,

María Quintana

B and C

Open tasks

Audio script

Task 1

1

I'm 35 years old and I really enjoy working on the Web. I use Macromedia Dreamweaver to design, develop, market and maintain web pages. For the last two years, I've been working for a successful TV company, where I'm responsible for updating their website regularly.

2

I started working in a computer support centre about three years ago. People phone and ask for help with things like: *my internet connection doesn't work, my hard drive has crashed, I think I've got a virus, I get a lot of error messages*, etc. I talk to the users, identify the problem and try to fix it. It's called troubleshooting.

3

I've got a degree in Electronic Engineering and I've now been with International Mercury Computers for two years. In my job, I design, develop and test computer components, microprocessors, sound boards, etc. I work closely with a software engineer to ensure that the software is compatible with the hardware.

4

I've been working for Novell, a leading provider of Net services software, since 2006. I plan and carry out measures to make networks more secure. In other words, I try to protect information from viruses and system crashes. I'm also in charge of assigning access passwords to employees.

Photocopiable © Cambridge University Press 2008

Audio script

Task 4

Mr Scott: I see you did a Computer Sciences degree at Aston University and did a work placement for a year with British Gas. What was that like?

Ms Brown: It was great. I really enjoyed it. It was really good to get some work experience and apply some of the ideas I was learning at college.

Mr Scott: And then you went to NCR. What did you do there?

Ms Brown: I worked as an analyst programmer for a year. I wrote software for general commercial use. The programs were for use on IBM mainframes.

Mr Scott: Right. That's good to know. And have you ever worked with databases?

Ms Brown: Yes, quite a bit. I usually work with Microsoft Access and dBase 5.

Mr Scott: Good. And what about your present job? What do you do at Intelligent Software?

Ms Brown: Well, I write programs in COBOL and C for commercial use. I write instructions, test the programs and prepare the documentation.

Mr Scott: That sounds the sort of experience we're looking for. What about foreign languages? Do you have any?

Ms Brown: Yes, I can speak Spanish and basic Italian. I've been studying Italian for the last eight months.

Mr Scott: Good. Just one more thing. Your current job sounds quite interesting. Why do you want to leave it?

Ms Brown: Well, I've been there for three years, and I want something more demanding and with more responsibility. I'd also like to learn about a new industry and have the chance to work with …

Photocopiable © Cambridge University Press 2008

8 Computers tomorrow

Learning objectives

In this module, you will:

- learn about different ICT systems.
- study the basics of networking.
- describe networks.
- learn and use phrasal verbs common in ICT.
- describe different game platforms and genres.
- give opinions about video games.
- learn and use adverbs.
- learn how to write a *For and Against* essay.
- make predictions about future trends.
- learn and use future forms.

Topic
Information and communication systems

Learning objectives
To write and talk about different ICT systems
To acquire specific vocabulary related to telecommunications
To understand how VoIP works

Language
Grammar: The passive
Vocabulary: ICT systems: *teletext, fax, digital TV, digital radio, call centre, GPS, teleworking, telemarketing, wireless, wearable computer, BlackBerry, cyborg*
VoIP: *ATA, Wi-Fi phone, spit*

Mobile phones: *LCD screen, brand, built-in camera, changeable faceplate, SIM card, wireless support, keypad, ringtone*

Skills
Listening: Understanding the most relevant information about VoIP, based on an interview
Speaking: Describing your mobile phone
Discussing the benefits and risks of using mobiles
Reading: Understanding general and specific information from a text about telecommunications
Writing: Writing a summary of a discussion about mobile phones

Optional materials
A mobile phone

Plan

Teacher's activities	Students' activities	Comments
Module page You may want to point out the learning objectives for your SS.	SS familiarize themselves with the topics and objectives of the Module.	
1 Information and communications technologies (ICT) **A** Elicit answers from SS and write the ICT systems suggested on the board. **B** Monitor the activity, helping where needed. **C** Do not give the answers for Task C yet, as SS will read for them in Task D. **D** Monitor the task, helping with any vocabulary problems. You may like to ask SS to find words with these prefixes, in the text: *tele-* (=over a distance): *television, telecommunications, telephone, teletext, teleworking, telemarketing* *trans-* (=across): *transmission* *inter-* (= between): *Internet, interactive* *intra-* (= within): *intranet*	**A** SS discuss the questions. **B** SS label pictures illustrating different ICT systems. **C** SS complete the sentences, using words from **B**. **D** SS read the article again and find specific information and vocabulary.	You may like to discuss these questions with SS: *What have been the most important advances in telecommunications over the last ten years? What will the future of telecommunications bring?*

2 Language work: the passive

A Refer SS to the HELP box, providing more examples if necessary. Ask SS to explain the differences between English and their mother tongue.

B Explain that the passive is very frequent in technical English and in journalism, as this text shows. Monitor the task, helping with any vocabulary problems.

C Monitor the task, helping where needed.

A SS explain how the passive is formed in their mother tongue and compare it with English.

B SS underline all the examples of the passive in the article and identify the tenses.

C SS complete the sentences with the correct passive forms.

3 VoIP technology

A Play track 33 of the CD and ask SS the question: *What is her prediction about the future of VoIP?*

B Play the CD again, pausing if necessary.

C Monitor the activity, helping where needed. You may like to set this as a written task instead.

A SS listen to an interview and answer the question.

B SS listen again and answer more questions.

C SS use a diagram to explain VoIP technology, in oral or written form.

You may like to give SS a copy of the audio script.

4 Mobile phones

A Instead of using the illustration, you may like to use a real mobile phone for this task.

B Refer SS to the *Useful language* box. Monitor the discussions, helping where needed.

C Monitor the discussions, helping where needed.

D You may like to set this task for homework.

A SS label the mobile phone with the correct features.

B In pairs, SS describe their mobile phones.

C SS discuss the questions in pairs.

D SS write a summary of the discussion in 80–90 words.

You may also like to bring some adverts or texts about mobile phones, discussing the features, advantages and disadvantages of mobile phones.

Evaluation of the unit:

Answer key

1 Information and communications technologies (ICT)

A

1 Possible answer

An ICT system is more than just a computer; it is a combination of hardware, software and data, and the people who use them. It often also includes communications technology, such as the Internet. Some ICT systems are used to manage data and information, others (for example, a mobile phone or an interactive TV) are used to send and receive text, voice and video content.

2 **Possible answers**

A computer network

Fax services

Teletext (a system of communicating information by using TV signals)

Public switched telephone network

Mobile phone network

Analogue and digital TV

Radio network

The Internet (email, the Web, Instant Messaging, FTP, etc.)

Satellite communications

3 One PC can be connected to another in the same building by using a Local Area Network (LAN). If the computers are further away from each other, they can be linked by adding modems and connecting them to the telephone lines (see Unit 28).

B

1	Teletext	5	Digital TV
2	Fax	6	Digital radio
3	Call centre	7	Wearable computer
4	GPS		

C

1	digital radio	5	call centre
2	Wearable computers	6	fax
3	digital TV	7	GPS
4	Teletext		

D

1 Modem
2 Teleworking
3 Broadcasting
4 It offers pay multimedia; it offers interactive services; it can be widescreen; it provides a better quality of picture and sound; you can have more channels
5 DMB (Digital Multimedia Broadcasting) and DVB-H (Digital Video Broadcast-Handheld)
6 Wireless
7 BlackBerrys
8 Cybernetic organism – a being that is part robot, part human

2 Language work: the passive

A

Open task

B

has been sent (present perfect), was arrested (past simple), had been caught (past perfect), was accused (past simple), (was) fined (past simple), is reported (present simple), has (now) been sentenced (present perfect), will be introduced (future)

C

1	are made	5	are being replaced
2	are used	6	will be accessed
3	have been equipped	7	can be connected
4	was developed	8	was being fixed

3 VoIP technology

A

She predicts that internet telephony (VoIP) will probably replace the traditional phone system and phone calls will eventually be free. She warns that some experts are concerned about security.

B

1 VoIP stands for Voice over Internet Protocol, a system which lets you make phone calls using the Internet instead of the regular phone line.
2 The recipient doesn't need any special equipment, just a phone.
3 An ATA is an analogue telephone adapter. Its function is to convert the analogue signals of your traditional phone into digital signals.
4 With a Wi-Fi phone, you are using the Internet, so the calls are free or at least much cheaper than using a mobile phone.
5 Yes, you need to have a VoIP service provider.
6 *Spit* is 'spam over internet telephony', for example unwanted voicemail messages.

C

Open task

4 Mobile phones

A

a Wireless support
b LCD screen
c Ringtone
d Changeable faceplate
e Keypad
f SIM card (Subscriber Identity Module)
g Built-in camera
h Brand

B, C and D

Open tasks

Audio script

Interviewer: Everybody says that VoIP will revolutionize the way we communicate today. But what exactly is 'VoIP'? To help me answer that question, I'm joined by Sue Reid, a specialist in telecommunications. Sue?

Sue: VoIP stands for Voice over Internet Protocol, a technology that lets you make phone calls using the Internet instead of the regular phone line.

Interviewer: And how does it work?

Sue: VoIP converts analogue voice into digital data and transmits it over the Internet with IP technology rather than via the traditional telephone network. When the data packets reach their final destination, they're converted into voice again. The person you're calling doesn't need any special equipment, just a phone.

Interviewer: But if I want to make a VoIP call, what sort of equipment do I need?

Sue: Well, you can make a call in three different ways. The easiest way is computer-to-computer. All you need is a program like Skype or DialPad, a microphone, speakers and a fast internet connection. You can download telephony software from the Net – it's even free – or you can make calls directly from a website.

Another way is through the use of a device called an ATA, an analogue telephone adapter, which converts the analogue signals of your traditional phone into digital signals. In this case you don't even need a computer. You just connect your telephone to the phone adapter, and the adapter to your broadband modem.

Thirdly, you can use a special VoIP phone with an Ethernet connector, which plugs directly into your internet connection. There are also wireless VoIP phones that let you make calls from any Wi-Fi access point – or hotspot – in many public locations. A Wi-Fi phone looks like a mobile phone, only it sends and receives audio signals via a wireless network.

Interviewer: But if I have a mobile phone, why use a Wi-Fi phone?

Sue: Well, with a Wi-Fi phone you're using the Internet, so the calls are free or at least much cheaper. And you don't have to pay roaming fees when you go abroad.

Interviewer: And do I need to have an account with a VoIP service provider?

Sue: Yes, you need a VoIP provider. They usually offer free calls to their subscribers and flat rates for other VoIP calls. Some providers charge a few cents for long distance calls.

Interviewer: What is the future of VoIP, in your opinion?

Sue: Some experts are concerned about security and predict that a new type of spam will appear; they call it *spit*, or *spam over internet telephony*. This means that our phones could be blocked with unwanted voice messages. But the future of internet telephony looks really promising. According to some industry analysts, internet telephony will probably replace the traditional phone system entirely and all phone calls will eventually be free.

Unit 28 | Networks

Topics
Networking basics
Types of network
Wired networks versus wireless networks

Learning objectives
To understand the basics of networking
To discuss the advantages of using networks
To describe networks, both in speaking and writing
To use phrasal verbs common in ICT

Language
Grammar: Verbs with particle (phrasal verbs)
Vocabulary: *wired network, wireless network, network architecture (client-server, peer-to-peer), network topology (bus, ring, star), protocol, router, Ethernet cables, fibre optic cable, wireless access point, Wi-Fi, Bluetooth*

Abbreviations: *PAN, LAN, MAN, WAN, GSM*
Phrasal verbs / verbs with particles: *look at, consist of, carry out, turn on/off, switch on/off, log in/on, log out /off, plug into, set up, sign up, try out, find out, take up, make up, fill in*

Skills
Listening: Labelling a diagram of a mixed wired/ wireless LAN based on information from a lecture
Speaking: Discussing the advantages of using networks
Describing a WAN connected via satellite
Reading: Understanding general and specific information from a text about networking
Writing: Describing a network

Technical help is given on page 127.

Plan

Teacher's activities	Students' activities	Comments
1 Small networks **A** Elicit ideas from SS and write them on the board. **B** Play track 34 of the CD. **C** Play the CD twice more if necessary.	**A** SS brainstorm ideas and try to define *computer network*. SS then discuss the benefits of using networks. **B** SS listen to the description of a LAN and answer the questions. **C** SS listen again and label the elements of the network.	You may like to write the word *network* on the board and elicit ideas about networks in real life: *TV network, telephone network, radio network, spy network, railway network, neural network, computer network*, etc. Make sure SS understand these basic concepts: *Local area network* (LAN), *wired* vs. *wireless, router, wireless access point*
2 Networking FAQs **A** Ask SS to only look at the FAQs for now. They will be reading the whole text in Task B. **B** Monitor the task, helping with any vocabulary problems. **C** Let SS do the network quiz in pairs or trios.	**A** SS look at the FAQs without reading the whole text and answer as many of them as they can. **B** SS read the whole text and find answers to the questions. **C** SS choose the correct answers in the network quiz.	You may like to set **C** as a game. The winners are the group that answers the most questions correctly in three minutes. Make sure SS understand the different ways of classifying networks.

3 Language work: phrasal verbs

A Refer SS to the HELP box, providing more examples if necessary. Encourage SS to explain how these verbs are formed in their mother tongue.

B and **C**
Monitor the tasks, helping where needed.

A SS study the HELP box and translate the phrasal verbs into their own language.

B SS complete some sentences with the correct form of phrasal verbs from the HELP box.

C SS then practise some phrasal verbs by matching questions and answers in short exchanges.

4 WANs and satellites

A Draw SS' attention to the picture and refer them to the *Useful language* box. Remind SS that this is a good opportunity to use the technical terms and the phrasal verbs learnt throughout the unit.
Encourage SS to prepare a PowerPoint presentation of the description.
Monitor the activity, helping where needed.

B Ask some students to present their description to the class.

A SS look at the illustration of a wide area network and then prepare a written description.

B Some SS present their description to the class, either as an oral report or as a PowerPoint presentation.

Evaluation of the unit:

Answer key

1 Small networks

A

Possible answers

1 A computer network is a system of interconnected computers that share files and other resources.

2 They enable us to get the most from our peripherals. For example, printers, scanners and high-speed modems or routers can be shared by a great number of users on the same network. In the same way, networks allow us to send and receive messages, have access to large databases, and transfer files to and from other computers. This implies faster communications, and flexible and interactive work between users.

B

1 Local Area Network

2 LANs are usually located within a relatively small geographical area, such as an office or building.

3 A wired LAN is connected with cables; a wireless LAN uses electromagnetic waves, such as radio waves, instead of cables.

C

1 mixed
2 Central computer (or File server)
3 cables
4 Broadband modem
5 Router
6 Wireless access point (or wireless router)

2 Networking FAQs

A

Open task

B

1 Personal Area Network
2 A network protocol is the language or set of rules that computers use to communicate with each other.
3 To log on to an Internet Service Provider, you need to type in your username and password.
4 WiMAX has greater range than Wi-Fi and is used to connect various Wi-Fi hotspots with each other. (WiMAX is short for Worldwide Interoperability for Microwave Access)
5 To set up a wireless LAN, you need computers equipped with a wireless adapter or wireless card, a wireless access point (a wireless router) and a broadband internet connection.
6 Wireless networks are easier to install; they let you move, or roam, from one access point to another. However, they are less secure than wired networks and are subject to interference.

C

1b   2a   3b   4c   5c   6b   7a   8c

3 Language work: verbs with particle

A

Open task

B

1 fill in
2 carries out
3 takes up
4 make up
5 find out

C

1c   2a   3e   4b   5d   6f

4 WANs and satellites

A

Possible answer

- The diagram represents a wide area network, or WAN, connecting two networks via satellite.
- The wired network in Barcelona is made up of a desktop PC and a PDA connected with Ethernet cables. A central computer acts as a file server, allowing the PCs to access common files and resources.
- The wireless network in Los Angeles consists of a wireless access point (a wireless router), which links multiple computers (a central computer, a laptop and a PDA) without using cables.
- In Barcelona, the network is connected by a modem to fibre optic cables. In Los Angeles, however, the computers are linked up by ordinary telephone lines.
- The satellite receives signals from a disk aerial. The signals are then amplified and sent on to workstations in Barcelona or Los Angeles.
- The purpose of this integrated network may be to establish information and communications services on a transcontinental scale. It allows large companies and institutions to exchange information, transfer files and communicate – for example, via videoconferencing – over long distances.

B

Open task

Audio script

Let's begin by talking about small networks, which are called local area networks, or LANs. These are groups of computers within a small physical area, like a home or an office building.

In this diagram, we see a mixed wired and wireless LAN, a typical solution for small businesses that already have a wired LAN and decide to expand it with wireless technologies to accommodate new needs.

In the existing fixed, wired LAN, the central computer is a file server with a large hard drive used to store common files and application programs. The computers, acting as clients, are connected to the file server and to a printer via Ethernet cables.

In the wireless part of the network, several devices, including desktops, laptops, PDAs and a gaming console, are connected to each other without cables. This part is controlled by a wireless access point – also called a wireless router. This access point is like a base station that transmits and receives radio frequencies from wireless-enabled devices. Each device that operates over the network is equipped with a wireless card or adapter.

Many wireless LANs use Wi-Fi, a wireless technology that uses radio waves to enable communication between devices in a limited area. This gives users flexibility and mobility. Another popular technology is Bluetooth, used for short distances.

The whole network is linked to the Internet via a broadband modem. This modem is plugged into a router, or hub, which splits the internet connection into parts and allows all users to access email and web resources. With appropriate networking software, users on the wireless LAN can share files and the printer located on the wired LAN.

Technical Help: Network topology

Topology refers to the shape of a network. There are three main topologies or configurations used in LANs:

In a **Star** network, all devices are connected to a central station, called a *star controller*. The central station functions as a switching centre. Computers cannot pass messages directly to one another; instead, they have to communicate via the central station, which prevents messages from colliding.

A **Bus** network consists of one cable to which all the devices are connected.

In a **Ring** network, all devices are connected to the same circuit, forming a continuous loop, or ring. A *token* (a piece of software) circulates continuously along the ring and is read through an adapter card in each machine as it passes by.

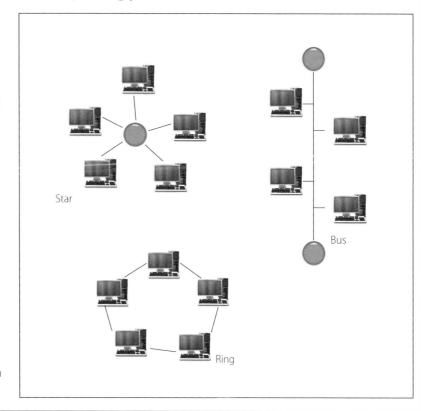

Star

Bus

Ring

Topics
Computer and video games
Gaming platforms and genres

Game genres: *First-person shooter, Action, Role-playing, Adventure, Puzzle, Sports, Racing, Simulation, Strategy, Fighting*

Learning objectives
To describe different game platforms and genres
To give opinions about video games
To use adverbs correctly
To write a *For and Against* essay

Language
Grammar: Adverbs
Vocabulary: Game platforms: *PC game, console game, arcade game, handheld game, mobile phone game, multiplayer online game*

Skills
Listening: Understanding the most relevant information about present and future trends in gaming from an interview
Speaking: Giving opinions about video games
Describing one's favourite video games to a partner
Reading: Understanding specific information about game platforms and genres from an article
Writing: An essay about the pros and cons of video games

Plan

Teacher's activities	Students' activities	Comments
1 Game platforms **A** Elicit SS' answers. **B** Draw SS' attention to the pictures. You may like to ask SS to talk about which of the types of game they have played in the past. **C** Monitor the task, helping with any vocabulary problems. **D** Monitor the discussions, helping where needed.	**A** SS discuss the questions. **B** SS match the types of game to the correct pictures. **C** SS complete short texts with the appropriate words from the box. **D** In pairs, SS discuss questions about game platforms and genres.	Make sure SS can distinguish between *game platforms* (electronic devices) and *game genres* (categories).
2 Game genres **A** Elicit SS' answers and write the list on the board. Ask SS to read the article and see if there are any genres mentioned that they did not think of. **B, C** and **D** Monitor the tasks, helping where needed.	**A** SS make a list of game genres and then read the article to see how many from their list are mentioned. **B** SS correct the false sentences. **C** SS look at the article again and find equivalent expressions. **D** In pairs, SS discuss the questions.	You may like to ask SS these questions: *Have you ever played any of the illustrated games? Do you use game screenshots as wallpaper for your computer desktop? If so, which games?*
3 Language work: adverbs **A** and **B** Refer SS to the HELP box, providing more examples if necessary.	**A** SS complete the sentences with adverbs made from the adjectives. **B** SS decide whether the words in bold are adjectives or adverbs.	Make sure that SS understand that not all words ending in *-ly* are adverbs.

4 Present and future trends in gaming

A Explain to SS that they are going to listen to an interview with a real blogger about the present and future trends in gaming. Play track 35 of the CD and ask the question: *How many game platforms does he mention?*

B Play the CD again, pausing if necessary.

C Play the CD a third time. Pause the CD after each extract so that SS can write the adverbs.

D Monitor the discussions, helping where needed.

A SS listen to the interview and answer the question.

B SS listen again and correct the false statements.

C SS listen again and complete the sentences with adverbs.

D SS discuss if they agree with Matt's predictions about the future of gaming. SS then make their own predictions.

You may like to give SS a copy of the audio script.

Matt Robinson is a real gaming blogger. SS may like to visit his blog at www.tpsreport.co.uk.

---

5 The pros and cons of gaming

A Monitor the discussions, helping where needed. Ask SS to justify their answers.
You may like to suggest that SS take notes during their discussions, as they will be writing about this topic in Task B.

B Refer SS to the *Useful language* box and the suggested structure for a *For and Against* essay.
You may like to set this task for homework.

A SS discuss the four questions.

B SS write an essay called *The pros and cons of video gaming*, using the steps provided.

Evaluation of the unit:

Answer key

1 Game platforms

A

Open task

B

a Handheld games
b PC games
c Console games
d Arcade games
e Massively multiplayer online games
f Mobile phone games

C

1 Console games; video game consoles
2 Handheld games; portable gaming devices
3 PC games; personal computer
4 Massively multiplayer online games
5 Mobile phone games; 3G mobile phones
6 Arcade games

D

Open task

2 Game genres

A

Open task

The following genres are mentioned in the text: First-person shooter (FPS), Action, Role-playing game (RPG), Massively multiplayer online RPGs, Adventure, Puzzle, Sports, Racing, Simulation, Strategy and Fighting.

B

1 **First-person shooter (FPS) and Action** games are currently the most popular.
2 Massively multiplayer online RPGs have been made possible by widespread **broadband** access.
3 *Oblivion* is a **Role-playing game**.
4 The *Sims* series is the **most** popular in the Simulation category.
5 Strategy games are mainly restricted to **PC**.
6 *Warcraft* belongs to the **Strategy** genre.
7 Console gamers typically prefer **Sports, Racing, Fighting, RPGs and a few FPS titles.**

C

1 currently	5 sub-genre
2 widespread	6 massive hits
3 despite	7 best-selling
4 increasingly	8 updated

D

Open task

3 Language work: adverbs

A

1 widely	4 well
2 recently	5 fast
3 mainly	

B

1 adj   2 adv   3 adj   4 adv   5 adv   6 adj

4 Present and future trends in gaming

A

Five: X-Box 360, Playstation 3, Nintendo Wii, Sony PSP and Nintendo DS

B

1 Video games are popular because **they are interactive, and players feel they are in control of the action.**
2 Well-known Hollywood actors **provide voices for the characters in video games.**
3 The Nintendo Wii is aimed at **families and groups of friends.**
4 It **isn't** free to play *World of Warcraft*. **Gamers need to subscribe and pay a fee.**
5 Holography is an advanced form of photography that uses lasers to produce **three-dimensional** images.
6 In the future, gesture recognition systems will **translate your head movements directly into the game.**

C

1 completely	5 currently
2 visually	6 entirely
3 certainly	7 traditionally
4 recently	

D

Open task

5 The pros and cons of gaming

A and B

Open tasks

Audio script

Interviewer: So, why do you think people play video games? Why are they so popular?

Matt: The great thing about video games is their interactivity. Compared to a more passive experience, such as watching a movie or reading a book, with a game you're completely in control of the action. With recent advances in graphics and hardware, games are now even more life-like and visually attractive.

Interviewer: The graphics in many games are so realistic that they almost look like films. What is the relationship between gaming and films? Do they influence each other?

Matt: A lot of modern games certainly draw inspiration from films and even TV. You can see it in the look of the characters, the sound of the dialogue, and in even more artistic elements such as lighting and camera work. The use of A-list Hollywood actors to provide voice work in games is no coincidence either and is a good example of the two media coming together.

Interviewer: And what's new? I mean, what are the top trends in the world of gaming?

Matt: Gaming is at a very interesting point right now. On the one hand you have the more cutting edge and flashy 'next generation' systems such as the Xbox 360 and the PlayStation 3, which opt more for that cinematic experience we were just talking about. Both are very attractive, but very expensive, machines designed solely for the more 'hardcore', or really dedicated, gamer. On the other hand, you have Nintendo taking gaming in a completely different direction. Their recently released 'Wii' console has an inexpensive, simplistic, 'pick up 'n' play' feel to it. Their goal is to provide a less serious, family experience that anyone can enjoy. Wii is currently the most popular of the three machines.

Interviewer: OK. And what about online multiplayer games? Is it feasible that millions of people will play and compete in a virtual world?

Matt: I would argue that this is already happening. Online gaming has become so popular that games like *World of Warcraft* are now taking in millions of pounds every month in subscription fees. Logging onto an entirely separate universe to meet and play alongside your friends has enormous attraction.

Interviewer: A lot of people play games on their mobile phones and portable devices. What's the future of mobile gaming?

Matt: Mobile gaming has traditionally been about easy, simplistic 2-D games, primarily to help people pass the time. However, with the release of portable devices such as the Sony PSP and the Nintendo DS, things are changing. Recent advances indicate that your mobile phone will soon include incredible 3-D graphics and CD-quality sound.

Interviewer: Now, imagine you're playing a video game ten years from now. Describe what it's like.

Matt: This year, I've seen companies demonstrating prototypes and ideas for future games. One company showed 3-D holographic images used for gaming purposes. Holography uses lasers and photographic plates to produce 3-D images, or holograms. Another company has a 'gesture recognition' system, which you simply attach to your head while you play. The idea is that your head movements are translated directly into the game. I think ten years from now we'll be playing fully photo-realistic games that look no different to what you see outside your window.

Topics
  Future trends
  New technologies: nanotechnology, artificial
    intelligence, biometrics, smart homes, ubiquitous
    computing, RFID tags

Learning objectives
  To talk and write about future trends in computing
  To make predictions about future trends
  To use future forms correctly

Language
  Grammar: Future forms: *will* + verb; *will be* + present
    participle; *will have* + past participle; *be going to* +
    verb
  Vocabulary: Nanotechnology: *nanometre,*
    nanocomputer, nanobot, nanomaterials, nanotube

Artificial intelligence (AI): *robot, android, expert*
system
Biometrics: *fingerprint, iris patterns*
Smart homes: *appliances, home area network, smart*
devices
Ubiquitous computing: *sensors, embedded*
RFID: *radio-frequency identification, tags*

Skills
  Listening: Understanding specific information about
    RFID tags from a class discussion
  Speaking: Discussing predictions about future trends
  Reading: Matching short texts with pictures
    Understanding the main features of new
    technologies from short texts
  Writing: Writing captions for pictures
    Making predictions about future trends

Plan

Teacher's activities	Students' activities	Comments
1 Future trends **A** Elicit SS' answers and write them on the board. **B** Encourage SS to read the texts quickly just to get a general idea. They will be reading them in more detail in Task C. **C** and **D** Monitor the tasks, helping with any vocabulary problems. **E** Write SS' suggested captions on the board and discuss them, perhaps asking SS to vote for whose are best.	**A** In pairs, SS discuss the questions. **B** SS match the texts with the pictures. **C** SS re-read the texts and find answers to the questions. **D** SS find words in the texts to match the definitions. **E** SS write captions for each picture in **B**.	Make sure SS understand these basic concepts: *nanobots, artificial intelligence, expert systems, biometrics, ubiquitous computing* and *smart homes*. Refer SS to the Glossary if necessary.
2 RFID tags **A** Tell SS they are going to listen to a teacher discussing RFID tags with her class. Play track 36 of the CD and ask SS to choose the best definition. **B** Read through the multiple-choice questions and then play the CD again, pausing if necessary. **C** Monitor the discussions, helping where needed. Ask SS to justify their answers.	**A** SS listen and decide which of the sentences is true. **B** SS listen again and choose the correct answers. **C** SS discuss how secure they think RFID is.	You may like to give SS a copy of the audio script.

3 Language work: future forms

A Refer SS to the HELP box, providing more examples if necessary. Make sure SS are able to distinguish between the future simple and the future with *going to*, which this task practises.

B Refer SS back to the HELP box. Make sure SS are able to distinguish between the forms and use of the future continuous and the future perfect.

C Monitor the discussions, encouraging SS to give arguments for and against.

4 Making predictions

A and **B**

Monitor the tasks, checking that SS are using the future tenses correctly. Encourage SS to be imaginative.

Online task

Visit www.cambridge.org/elt/ict for an online task related to the topic of this module.

A SS choose the correct future form in brackets.

B SS complete the sentences with the correct future tense.

C In pairs or small groups, SS discuss a list of predictions and say if they agree or disagree.

A SS write their own predictions about the four topics.

B SS discuss and compare their predictions in pairs, finding out more information.

You may like to write the most original predictions on the board.

Evaluation of the unit:

Answer key

1 Future trends

A

1 In this context, *trend* refers to new developments or changes.

2 Open task

B

a2   b1   c3   d5   e4

C

1 Nanometre (one billionth of a metre)

2 Nanotubes are more flexible, resistant and durable than regular materials such as steel or aluminium.

3 Doctors will use expert systems to diagnose illnesses.

4 Biometrics analyse physical characteristics, such as fingerprints, facial features, voice, iris and retina patterns.

5 Ubiquitous computing or pervasive computing

6 The alarm system will alert the alarm company and then the police. It will also turn on the lights in the home and then send a text message to the owner's phone. It may even send images captured by wireless cameras to phones and PCs.

7 All devices will be interconnected over a home area network.

D

1 nanobot

2 android

3 biometrics

4 embedded

5 appliances

E

Possible answers

a Robots and androids – artificial intelligence in the image of man

b Nanotechnology – the next computer revolution

c   Biometric solutions for human identification
d   Smart homes – intelligent homes for the 21st century
e   Ubiquitous computing – smart devices integrated into our lives and communicating with each other wirelessly

2 RFID tags

A

b

B

1a   2b   3a   4a   5b   6a

C

Open task

3 Language work: future forms

A

1	'll have	4	'll lend
2	're going to spill	5	will probably change
3	're going to give	6	will be

B

1	will have found	4	will have bought
2	will be living	5	will be living
3	will be working		

C

Open task

4 Making predictions

A and B

Open tasks

Audio script

Sarah: OK everyone, today we're looking at RFID tags. Does anyone know what RFID is?

Student 1: Isn't it a radio technology?

Sarah: Yes, that's right. RFID stands for Radio Frequency Identification. It uses microchips, smaller than a grain of sand, to store and transmit data using radio waves. These chips are called radio tags and can be attached to a product, animal, or person for the purpose of identification.

Student 2: And how does it work?

Sarah: There are two types of radio tag. Passive RFID tags are so called because they have no power supply. They have an antenna that receives energy from a reader device and can only be read at short distances – up to five metres. Active RFID tags, on the other hand, come with a battery that provides internal power and have practical ranges of several hundred metres.

Student 3: And what sort of data is stored on the chip?

Sarah: Most tags used to track products like clothes or books only contain a unique identification number, similar to a bar code. But the chips being implanted into passports can store data such as name, address, nationality, sex, as well as biometric data like iris patterns or fingerprints. Radio tags can also be attached to animals and everyday items. That means you'll be able to find your dog, glasses or car keys when they're lost.

Student 1: I've heard they can be used in humans as well.

Sarah: Yes, RFID chips can be inserted under the skin. For example, some nightclubs are using an implantable chip to identify their customers, who then use it to pay for drinks. Some hospitals are implanting chips into patients' arms, so that hospital staff can access their medical records. Another company is working on an implant that will contain a GPS. A device like that would allow us to pinpoint someone's position on the globe.

Student 2: It sounds like this technology might change our lives completely.

Sarah: It probably will. But can anyone think of any potential problems with RFID?

Student 3: Security risks or privacy concerns?

Sarah: Exactly. Consumer organizations say that tags might be used to track people to their homes after they've left the shop. Another risk is from hackers, who might steal another person's identity. But manufacturers say we needn't worry, because they're developing encryption systems to protect radio tags from unauthorized scanning, and the tags embedded into humans will be easily removable.

Photocopiable © Cambridge University Press 2008

A Vocabulary

1 Match the verbs (1–6) with the nouns (a–f) to make common collocations.

1 make   a information
2 store   b ringtones
3 keep   c video calls
4 access   d records
5 dispense   e the Internet
6 download   f money

1 mark for each correct answer   **Total _/6**

2 Use the collocations from 1 to complete these sentences.

1 They use a database to _____ _____ of customers, suppliers and orders.
2 Using the built-in camera, you can _____ _____ to other 3G mobile phones and see yourself and the person you're talking to on the screen.
3 I _____ _____ using Wi-Fi when I'm travelling.
4 If both card and PIN are valid, the ATM will proceed to _____ _____ to the customer.
5 Windows and Mac OS both use different formats to _____ _____ on disk.
6 Most mobile phones allow you to _____ _____ , music and wallpapers.

2 marks for each correct answer   **Total _/12**

3 Match the terms (1–6) with their definitions (a–f).

1 mainframe ☐
2 input ☐
3 processing ☐
4 output ☐
5 disk drive ☐
6 port ☐

a The visible and audible result of data processing
b A connection point for a peripheral device
c A device that enables the computer to read and write data on disks
d Performing operations on data, such as calculating, editing, drawing and searching
e Data fed into a computer for processing
f A large, powerful computer, often serving many connected terminals

2 marks for each correct answer   **Total _/12**

B Language work

4 Complete the definitions 1–5 using relative pronouns (*who, which, that*) and the information in a–e.

1 The CPU is a chip _____
2 A hacker is a person _____
3 A modem is an electronic device _____
4 A software engineer is someone _____
5 The mobile phone is a device _____

a it enables a computer to communicate with another over telephone lines
b he/she writes computer programs
c people use for communicating with each other
d it acts as the brain of a computer
e he/she invades a network's privacy

2 marks for each correct answer   **Total _/10**

5 Match the extracts from the dialogue in 6 (1–7) with the language functions that they are expressing (a–g).

1 *They're both very fast* ☐
2 *we're looking for a portable computer* ☐
3 *how much do they cost?* ☐
4 *has a 15.4" LCD screen* ☐
5 *you're obviously getting a faster computer, with more memory* ☐
6 *Do you need any help?* ☐
7 *What's the storage capacity of the hard disk?* ☐

a Offering help
b Explaining what you are looking for
c Asking for technical specs
d Giving technical specs
e Describing
f Comparing
g Asking the price

1 mark for each correct answer   **Total _/7**

6 Complete this dialogue with the extracts from Exercise 5 (1–7).

Assistant: Good morning. (1) _____ ?
George: Um, yes, (2) _____ . Have you got any basic laptops?
Assistant: Yes. At the moment we've got these two models: The Lenovo ThinkPad R60 notebook, which has an Intel Core 2 Duo processor running at 1.83 gigahertz, and the Toshiba Satellite A205, a laptop with a processor operating at 2.0 gigahertz. (3) _____ and reliable.
Annie: And which has the most RAM?

Assistant:	Well, the ThinkPad has 1,024MB, which can be expanded up to 3GB, and the Toshiba Satellite has 2,048MB, expandable to 4GB.
Annie:	Right. (4) _____ ?
Assistant:	The ThinkPad has a capacity of 160GB, and the Toshiba Satellite's hard drive can hold 250GB.
Annie:	And what about the screen? Is there any difference?
Assistant:	The ThinkPad notebook (5) _____ , and the Toshiba comes with a 17" widescreen monitor. Both have a camera built right into the display, for video chats.
Annie:	And (6) _____ ?
Assistant:	The ThinkPad costs £749 and the Toshiba Satellite is £1,099. For that price (7) _____ and a larger screen.
Paul:	Do they come with Windows Vista pre-installed?
Assistant:	Yes, they both come with the Home Premium version; they also include internet software, Wi-Fi, and Bluetooth support.
Paul:	OK, well, thanks very much. We need to go away and think about it.

2 marks for each correct answer   **Total ___/14**

C Reading

7 Read the text and then answer these questions.

1 What sort of power supply does a PDA use?
2 What kind of screen do PDAs have?
3 How do you write characters with a stylus if the PDA doesn't include handwriting recognition?
4 What are the four major operating systems for PDAs?
5 What sort of things can you do with a PDA?
6 What are the limitations or disadvantages of handheld computers over standard PCs?
7 How can you exchange data between a PDA and a standard PC?

2 marks for each correct answer   **Total ___/14**

How do PDAs work?

A PDA (personal digital assistant) is a handheld organizer with phone and internet capabilities. PDAs are also called palmtops and pocket PCs. They run on batteries.

PDAs vary in how you input data and instructions. Some devices use a stylus to write, draw or make selections on a touch-sensitive LCD screen. Software inside the PDA recognizes hand-written characters and converts them into editable text. If the device doesn't incorporate handwriting recognition, you use the stylus to tap on the letters of a miniature on-screen keyboard. In addition, many devices now include a small QWERTY keyboard. They may also have a speech recognition system, which reacts to the user's voice, and a few buttons to launch programs and scroll through the files.

As for the operating system, most PDAs run on Windows Mobile or Palm OS. However, BlackBerry wireless devices use RIM, from Research In Motion, and Nokia and Samsung smartphones use the Symbian OS. A smartphone is a full-featured mobile phone with PDA capabilities.

Today's PDAs come with PIM software that lets you manage personal information, such as contacts, appointments and to-do lists. They can be used as a radio or MP3 player, play games, record voice and video, act as GPS devices, and connect to the Internet through Wi-Fi access points or cellular data networks. Some PDAs can also run pocket versions of MS Word, Excel, a web browser and an email program.

PDA processors are smaller, cheaper and less powerful than those in standard PCs. A widely used microprocessor is ARM, based on a RISC (reduced instruction set computer) architecture, which reduces chip complexity by using simpler instructions.

Unlike standard computers, PDAs don't have a hard disk; they store the basic programs (operating system, calendar, calculator, etc.) in a ROM chip. The programs that you add and the data being processed are held in the RAM chips. The newest PDAs use flash memory instead of RAM. Flash memory is non-volatile – i.e. it retains its information when the power is off. Flash memory cards are ideal for storing the user's favourite music, picture and video files.

Most models can synchronize to a PC – i.e. exchange data and update it – in case you want to access the same data on both devices. To synchronize and transfer data, you need to connect your PDA to a standard PC via a USB cable or wirelessly. Modern devices support two types of wireless connections: IrDA, which uses infrared light beams similar to TV remote controls, and Bluetooth, which uses radio waves to communicate over short distances with Bluetooth-enabled devices (laptops, mobiles, etc.).

8 Find words in the text with the following meanings.

1 a special pen used as an input device on a pressure-sensitive screen _____
2 the process of converting spoken words into text or commands _____
3 a mobile phone with computing functions _____
4 a satellite navigation system _____
5 a computer architecture that uses a limited number of instructions _____
6 a type of memory that holds its content without power _____
7 having no wires _____

1 mark for each correct answer   **Total ___/7**

D Writing

9 Draw a diagram of the hardware and software components of your computer. Then describe the components and their functions. Use classifying expressions (e.g. *consists of ... , includes ... , ... are classified into X types*).

Total ___/18

TOTAL A+B+C+D ___ / 100

A Vocabulary

1 Which device (a–h) would you use for the tasks (1–8)?

1 to show data on the screen ☐
2 to capture moving images and then download them to the computer ☐
3 to read price labels on products sold in shops ☐
4 to read text or pictures from paper and transfer the information onto the computer ☐
5 to type text into a computer ☐
6 to select menu options, text and graphics displayed on the monitor ☐
7 to send live video images via the Internet ☐
8 to enter drawings and sketches into the computer ☐

a scanner
b monitor
c webcam
d bar code reader
e graphics tablet
f digital video camera
g keyboard
h mouse

1 mark for each correct answer   **Total _ / 8**

2 Complete each sentences using the word in brackets and one of these suffixes.

Adjective suffixes: *-ful, -less, -ive, -ed, -al, -y, -ic*

Noun suffixes: *-tion, -er, -ing, -logy, -ness*

1 We are the world's leading _____ of digital cameras for professional photographers. (manufacture)
2 We offer the most advanced _____ in printing services. (techno)
3 The amount of light produced by an LCD screen is called _____ , or luminance, measured in cd/m2. (bright)
4 A _____ mouse has no cable, and an optical mouse has no ball. (wire)
5 This camcorder will give you rich, _____ pictures, thanks to its CMOS sensor. (colour)
6 A digital camera uses a digital image sensor instead of _____ film. (photograph)
7 New digital cameras offer _____ features such as Bluetooth connectivity. (innovate)

1 mark for each correct answer   **Total _/7**

3 Complete the gaps with words from the box.

| pixels | magnifier | ergonomics | widescreen |
| Braille | textphone | | |

1 A screen _____ enlarges text and graphics on the screen, increasing the legibility.
2 The universal system of writing and printing for the blind is called _____ .
3 A _____ has a screen and a keyboard that transcribes spoken voice as text; it is ideal for deaf people.
4 A _____ display has an aspect ratio of 16:9, ideal for watching movies.
5 Characters and pictures are made up of coloured dots, also called _____ .
6 Computer _____ refers to the position of your body in relation to the computer, including the chair, the desk and the monitor.

2 marks for each correct answer   **Total _/12**

4 What do these abbreviations stand for?

1 LCD _____
2 CRT _____
3 RSI _____
4 dpi _____
5 WAI _____
6 USB _____

1 mark for each correct answer   **Total _/6**

B Language work

5 Describe the use of these devices.

A digital camera

Example: *A digital camera is used to take and store images as digital (binary) data, which can then be processed by a PC.*

1 A printer
_____
_____
_____
_____

2 A touch screen
_____
_____
_____
_____

3 A game controller
_____
_____
_____
_____

4 marks for each correct answer   **Total _/12**

6 Complete these sentences using the comparative or superlative form of the adjectives in brackets.

1 Laser printers are usually (fast) _____ than inkjets, printing text pages at a speed of 10 to 20 ppm, and are (cheap) _____ to operate.

2 The human brain is far (powerful) _____ than the (advanced) _____ computer working at its full capacity.

3 I recommend getting the (high) _____ resolution monitor you can afford.

4 Plasma screens are (heavy) _____ than LCD screens.

5 The ILOVEYOU computer bug is the (bad) _____ virus in history.

6 Film scanners are (expensive) _____ than flatbeds, usually starting at £250.

7 This printer has been ranked as the (less reliable) _____ on the market.

1 mark for each correct answer　　　　**Total __/9**

7 Explain these noun phrases.

Example: disk controller = *a chip that controls a disk drive*

1 A speech recognition system

_____

2 A voice-activated computer

_____

3 The teacher's laptop

_____

4 A drawing and painting program

_____

2 marks for each correct answer　　　　**Total __/8**

C Reading

8 Read the text and find the following.

1 a type of interface that allows users to select things by clicking on icons and menus _____

2 the technique which uses a computer model or program to reproduce a particular situation _____

3 a device used to manipulate and move virtual objects with your hands _____

4 devices which contain movement sensors _____

5 the machines that simulate flying conditions _____

6 machines designed to operate in dangerous environments _____

2 marks for each correct answer.

Total __ / 12

Virtual reality devices

The most common user interface in computing today is a graphical user interface, or GUI. Typically, a GUI includes menus, windows, icons, buttons and a mouse as pointing device. But with the development of virtual reality (VR) techniques, a different type of interface has emerged: a virtual interface. VR uses 3-D graphics and computer simulation to generate an imaginary world in which the user can move.

In a virtual interface, you put on a head-mounted display (HMD) to see the pictures, which makes you feel as if you are in a 3-D world. Most HMDs have two displays and provide stereoscopic vision.

You also use sophisticated controlling devices, such as 3-D joysticks, gloves, special suits and motion detectors. A virtual mouse, trackball or joystick is used to move around the space you are exploring. A data glove (or VR glove) has pressure pads and sensors on the fingers which make you feel as if you are picking up objects and touching things. Full body suits with position and bend sensors are used for capturing motion. Motion detectors allow the machine to sense when and how you move.

VR systems are already being used in fields like video games, architectural design and virtual exhibitions. Other VR applications allow participants to view reality from an advantageous position, for example simulators and telepresence systems. In simulators, scientists recreate a particular condition or situation by using a computer program to reproduce it. For example, pilots use flight simulators to do their training. A telepresence system connects remote sensors in the real world with the senses of a person; for instance, doctors use tiny cameras and instruments on cables to do complicated surgery, and scientists use remotely operated robots to work in dangerous conditions, to explore volcanic activity, the depths of the ocean, or outer space.

9 Find the words in the text with the following meanings.

1 artificial reality or environment generated by computers

_____

2 user interface based on virtual reality

_____

3 a video display that a person wears in front of the face

_____

4 effect of perceiving a 3-D world by sending two views to the user's right and left eyes

_____

5 control device used in video games

_____

6 very small

_____

1 mark for each correct answer　　　　**Total __/6**

D Writing

10 You have read this post on a forum. Write a response, describing the advantages and disadvantages of the two options.

"I need to scan and print all sorts of text and graphic documents. Should I get a multifunction printer or a separate printer and a scanner?"

Total __ / 20

TOTAL A+B+C+D ___/ 100

A Vocabulary

1 Match the words (1–7) with the definitions (a–g).

1 floppy disk drive ☐
2 formatting ☐
3 seek time ☐
4 defragmenter ☐
5 USB flash drive ☐
6 CD/DVD burner ☐
7 data transfer rate ☐

a The average time required for the read/write head to move and access data on a magnetic disk

b The process of initializing a disk and preparing it to receive data

c The average speed with which data can be transmitted from the disk to the CPU, measured in megabytes per second

d A small portable drive that plugs into a computer's port; also called a *pen drive* or *key drive*

e A program that helps you reorganize broken up files into continuous sectors on the hard disk

f A storage device that uses 3.5" diskettes

g A storage device that writes data to optical discs

2 marks for each correct answer   **Total __/14**

2 Solve the clues and complete the puzzle.

ACROSS

1 Portable hard drives are used to make a _____ of important files or to transport data between PCs.

4 PCs usually have one hard _____ , called C.

6 DVD-RW means Digital Versatile Disc - _____ .

7 Non-_____ memory is computer memory that can retain the stored information even when not powered.

DOWN

2 Flash memory _____ are used to store information in digital cameras and other handheld devices.

3 Unit of memory equivalent to 1,024 megabytes

5 When a disk is formatted, its surface is divided into concentric circles known as _____ .

2 marks for each correct answer   **Total __/14**

B Language work

3 Complete these sentences with *should/shouldn't* or nothing (–).

1 You _____ write on discs with permanent pens.

2 Don't _____ hit or move the computer while the hard disk is spinning.

3 You _____ update your anti-virus program regularly.

4 You _____ turn your PC on and off quickly. Wait a few seconds to ensure that its internal components have stopped working.

2 marks for each correct answer   **Total __/8**

4 Choose the correct connectors in brackets to complete these sentences.

1 A virus entered my computer. (As a result / On the other hand), many files have been destroyed.

2 DVD-R and DVD+R can record data once, (therefore / whereas) DVD-RW and DVD+RW can be rewritten thousands of times.

3 Many software companies support the Business Software Alliance, an anti-piracy group, (besides / because) software piracy is a problem that costs the industry millions of pounds a year.

4 (Moreover / Although) Blu-ray and HD-DVD players are backward compatible with all CD and DVD formats, they are not compatible with each other.

2 marks for each correct answer

Total __/8

5 Choose the correct words in brackets to complete these sentences.

1 We need more money to (compute / computerize / computational) the school library.

2 Today, most of the information we produce is stored (digital / digitizing / digitally).

3 Information is stored on a magnetic disk in the form of (magnetized / magnetically / magnetizable) spots, called bits.

4 As you use your PC, the hard disk becomes (defragmented / fragmenting / fragmented) – files are broken up into small pieces that are stored at different locations across the drive.

5 The set of all weblogs on the Internet is called the (blogging / blogosphere / blogsphere).
6 The Apple iPhone combines three products – a mobile phone, a widescreen iPod, and an internet device – into one small (handhold / handheld / handhelded) device.
7 The iPhone also features 8GB of flash storage, Bluetooth for short-range (wireless / wirelessly / wired) communications, Wi-Fi for internet access, and a 2-megapixel camera.

2 marks for each correct answer   **Total _/14**

C Reading

6 Match the headlines (1–3) with the correct extracts (a–c).

1 Hybrid drives promise faster laptops and PCs
2 New 4x burner and BD-R discs
3 Moving closer to the terabyte era

2 marks for each correct answer   **Total _/6**

a _____

Samsung Electronics announces the SpinPoint F1, a hard drive with a storage capacity of 1TB. The new F1 series features the world's highest recording density in a 3.5" hard disk drive, using only three disks.

The SpinPoint F1 1TB drive consists of three 334GB platters, enough space to store more than 300,000 6-megapixel images, 250,000 MP3s or 1,000 hours of standard definition video. It features a spin speed of 7,200 rpm and an average seek time of 8.9 ms. It also uses Perpendicular Magnetic Recording (PMR), a process that achieves higher storage densities and ensures recording stability.

The F1 also comes with disk utilities such as formatting, partition, compression and defragmentation software.

Samsung plans to sell the F1 Series for about $390.

b _____

Major storage manufacturers, such as Seagate, Samsung and Hitachi, have launched hybrid drives that integrate a 1.5" magnetic hard disk with up to 256MB of on-board flash memory.

With the hybrid HDD, manufacturers seek to combine the benefits of both technologies: magnetic hard drives offer low cost and extraordinary storage; flash memory offers speed and reliability. Flash memory is used as a non-volatile disk cache, a mechanism that allows quick access to data so that it can be retrieved faster, reducing the use of the hard disk, thus cutting power consumption.

The first computer with a hybrid hard drive was the Samsung R55 notebook, followed by the LG R400. The new generation of PCs will probably run faster and last longer thanks to these hybrid hard drives and a feature in the Windows Vista operating system, called ReadyDrive, that uses NAND flash memory as a disk cache.

c _____

Panasonic has developed a new drive capable of writing to Blu-ray discs at 4x speed. The new discs are available in both 25GB and 50GB, which allows consumers to conveniently handle large amounts of data and high-definition content.

The Blu-ray disc system uses a blue-violet laser operating at a wavelength of 405 nm (nanometers) to read and write data. Conventional DVDs, however, use red lasers at 650 nm. A dual layer Blu-ray disc can store 50GB, almost six times the size of a dual layer DVD at 8.5GB. Blu-ray is particularly well-suited to high-definition films and video games. Blu-ray players are backward-compatible with CD/DVD formats.

7 Read the texts again and answer these questions.

1 What is the average access time of the SpinPoint F1 drive?
_____
2 Which technology allows a hard drive to increase its capacity for data? _____
3 What are the benefits of using flash memory in a hybrid hard drive? _____
4 Which company first released a laptop with a hybrid hard drive? _____
5 Where does the Blu-ray format get its name?
_____
6 What is the storage capacity of a dual layer Blu-ray disc?
_____

2 marks for each correct answer   **Total _/12**

8 Find words in the texts with the following meanings.

1 unit of memory equivalent to 1,024GB _____
2 magnetic disks that constitute part of a hard drive _____
3 software used for performing disk-related tasks, such as formatting, partitioning and defragmenting _____
4 a storage device that combines a magnetic hard disk drive and flash memory _____
5 a portion of memory used to speed up access to data
_____
6 acronym for *light amplification by stimulated emission of radiation* _____
7 describes devices that can play back previous formats
_____

2 marks for each correct answer   **Total _/14**

D Writing

9 Write an email to a friend, recommending a new flash-based media player (e.g. an MP3 player) that you have seen in a computer shop.

Total _ / 10

TOTAL A+B+C+D ___/ 100

A Vocabulary

1 Match the GUI features (1–8) with the pictures (a–h).

1 pointer ☐
2 drop-down menu ☐
3 menu bar ☐
4 document icon ☐
5 folder ☐
6 program icon ☐
7 scroll bar ☐
8 command button ☐

a   🍎 **Finder File Edit View Go Window Help**

b ▮   c Next ›

d

e

g   Network / Macintosh HD / Desktop / user / Applications / Documents / Movies / Music

f

h

1 mark for each correct answer   **Total __/8**

2 Which type of software (1–7) would be most suitable for the office tasks (a–g)?

1 spreadsheet program ☐
2 database management system ☐
3 word processor ☐
4 videoconferencing program ☐
5 business accounting package ☐
6 email package ☐
7 presentation program ☐

a to write letters and faxes
b to handle accounts and organize wages, taxes, payments, etc.
c to make calculations in the form of mathematical tables
d to store, manipulate and retrieve data
e to exchange messages with clients and colleagues
f to display information in the form of a slide show
g to create virtual meetings over long distances so that the participants can see and hear each other

1 mark for each correct answer   **Total __/7**

3 Match the word processing functions (1–8) with the correct icons (a–h).

1 Cut and Paste ☐
2 Increase Indent ☐
3 Insert Picture ☐
4 Insert Hyperlink ☐
5 Align Right ☐
6 Bullets ☐
7 Print Preview ☐
8 Undo ☐

a   b   c   d

e   f   g   h

1 mark for each correct answer   **Total __/8**

4 Complete these sentences with words from the box.

column	query	row	record	formulae
cell	field			

1 In a spreadsheet, each _____ is identified with a letter at the top.
2 Each _____ of the spreadsheet is labelled with a number at the left.
3 The point where a column and a row intersect is called a _____ .
4 A cell can hold three types of information: text, numbers and _____ .
5 A database _____ consists of a number of interrelated data elements, called fields.
6 In a database, a _____ stores a single piece of information of a particular data type. Examples are NAME, ADDRESS and DEPARTMENT.
7 A _____ function lets you extract data according to certain criteria.

1 mark for each correct answer   **Total __/7**

B Language work

5 Correct the mistakes in these sentences.

1 I need an advice on which computer to buy.
_____

2 If some informations are inaccurate, please tell me.
_____

3 There are much Windows versions.
_____

4 Sarah often uses a laptop to do her homeworks.
_____

5   I spent a few time playing around with the program.

_____

1 mark for each correct answer   **Total __/5**

6 Complete this text with *a, an, the* or nothing (–).

In our classroom, we have five computers connected to (1) _____ Internet. We use them to prepare (2) _____ projects and reports, and to study subjects like (3) _____ Music, Art and Science. This year, we are preparing (4) _____ exchange with students from a partner school in Europe.

Our teachers use (5) _____ video projector to make (6) _____ presentations on a large screen. At home I have a desktop PC and (7) _____ inkjet printer. I use my computer to play games, send and receive (8) _____ email, and get (9) _____ information from (10) _____ Web.

1 mark for each correct answer   **Total __/10**

7 Write the plural of these words.

1 business _____	6 switch _____
2 software _____	7 woman _____
3 technology _____	8 child _____
4 analysis _____	9 formula _____
5 tax _____	10 query _____

1 mark for each correct answer   **Total __/10**

8 Put these instructions into the correct order.

How to copy a picture from a web page

☐ Move your cursor over the picture and right click. A pop up menu will appear on the screen. Choose *Copy* to copy the image onto the Clipboard.

☐ First, find the picture that you want to insert as an illustration in a Word document.

☐ Next, switch to your Word document and click where you want to insert the image.

☐ Once the picture has been pasted, you may like to resize it and move it to a different location.

☐ Then choose *Edit* on the Menu bar at the top of the screen, and click *Paste*. This will insert the picture at the insertion point.

1 mark for each correct answer   **Total __/5**

C Reading

9 Read the text and decide whether these sentences are true or false. Correct the false ones.

1   A graphic suite lets you create documents, spreadsheets and presentations.

_____

2   The dominant office suite is currently *Microsoft Office*.

_____

3   IBM *Lotus SmartSuite* is free to download, use and distribute.

_____

4   *OpenOffice* users can share documents with Microsoft users.

_____

2 marks for each correct answer   **Total __/8**

Basic office software

Most businesses use office suites to create text documents, spreadsheets and presentations. An office suite, or productivity suite, is a collection of programs that are sold as a package and perform essential office functions.

Application office suites usually combine a word processor, a spreadsheet program and a presentation program, but they can also contain a database manager, an email client, a web browser, Instant Messaging, collaboration groupware, and a personal information manager, or PIM, which includes a calendar, task manager, address book, and more. Each edition has is own mix of programs and utilities, and each component can be installed separately.

The most widely used office suite is *Microsoft Office*, a standard in office software. Depending on the edition, it includes some combination of *Word*, the *Excel* spreadsheet program, the *PowerPoint* presentation program, the *Access* database manager, the *Outlook* mail program, along with various internet and other utilities. Another popular proprietary suite is *IBM Lotus SmartSuite*, which includes *WordPro*, the famous *Lotus 1-2-3* spreadsheet, *Freelance Graphics* for business presentations, *Approach* relational database, and *Lotus Organizer*.

One alternative to proprietary packages is *OpenOffice*, a free, open-source suite available under the GNU Lesser General Public Licence, which means anyone can use it or modify it for their own purposes. *OpenOffice* includes *Writer*, *Calc*, *Impress* and *Draw*, among other components. Other competitors are online office suites such as *Google Apps* and *ThinkFree Office*; these web-based programs allow subscribers to do the typical office things, collaborate on documents with others, and even publish to a blog or website.

The components of a suite have a consistent graphical user interface (GUI) and can exchange data with each other. The OLE (object linking and embedding) feature allows users to insert information from one program into another. The object may be *linked*, reflecting the changes that users make to the original, or just *embedded* – inserted as a static copy of the original. Objects can also be dragged and dropped between applications.

Office suites are available for most operating systems, including Windows, Linux and Mac OS. *Lotus SmartSuite* and *OpenOffice* are compatible with Microsoft Office – i.e. they can read Word or Excel files, and even save files in Microsoft formats (.doc for text documents, .xls for spreadsheets, .ppt for presentations, etc.). Office suites are reasonably secure, as long as you have an anti-virus program, and may include a document recovery tool that helps you retrieve documents after a system failure.

10 Read the text again and then answer these questions.

1 What are the typical components of an office suite?

_____

2 What is the advantage of using *OpenOffice*?

_____

3 What type of user interface is shared by the components of an office suite?

_____

4 How can you retrieve documents after a system crash?

_____

2 marks for each correct answer   **Total _/8**

11 Find the following in the text.

1 a package which contains all the main functions needed within a typical office environment _____

2 another name for office suites _____

3 a category of software designed to help groups work together _____

4 describes a database in which tables have a connection or link with one another _____

5 a technology that allows objects such as a graphic or video clip to be linked or embedded into a document

_____

6 the set of programs that control the hardware and software of a computer system _____

1 mark for each correct answer   **Total _/6**

D Writing

12 Summarize the text on the previous page in 75–80 words.

Total _/18

TOTAL A+B+C+D ___/ 100

Test | Module 5

A Vocabulary

1 Choose the correct answers.

1 The language used for data transfer on the Internet is called
   a HTTP.   **b** TCP/IP.   **c** ADSL.

2 Which device is used to connect a computer to the telephone network?
   a modem   **b** USB connector   **c** hub

3 If you want to connect multiple computers to the Internet without using cables, you need a
   a wired router.   **b** modem.   **c** wireless router.

4 Which technology lets you have real-time conversations online, by typing messages?
   a VoIP   **b** Telnet   **c** Instant Messaging

5 What is a collection of web pages called?
   a the Internet   **b** a website   **c** a homepage

6 This technique encodes data so that unauthorized users can't read the information.
   a decryption   **b** encryption   **c** firewall

7 The fraudulent attempt to steal passwords and personal data, usually via email, is known as
   a phishing.   **b** piracy.   **c** IP spoofing.

1 mark for each correct answer   **Total __/7**

2 Match the parts of these internet addresses (1–8) with the descriptions (a–h).

kroberts1943@yahoo.co.uk

1 _____   2 _____   3 _____

http://www.cambridge.org/elt/infotech/about.htm/

4 _____   5 _____ 6 _____ 7 _____ 8 _____

a   domain name of the mail server
b   username
c   the protocol used to connect to web servers
d   the directory path; the place where the web page is located
e   domain name of the web server
f   the name of a single web page
g   the symbol that means *at*
h   also known as W3 (short for World Wide Web)

1 mark for each correct answer   **Total __ / 8**

3 Solve the clues and complete the puzzle.

1   Also called a smiley, an expression of emotion typed into a message

2   A text or image that, when clicked, takes you to other destination on the Web

3   A popular website that allows users to view and share video clips

4   The buying and selling of products on the Internet

5   Word derived from *malicious software*

6   High-speed transmission, commonly referring to internet access via cable or ADSL

7   People who use technology for criminal aims; also called *black hats* or *darkside hackers*

8   An icon or representation of a user in games and chat rooms

9   An audio broadcast distributed over the Net

10 Unsolicited junk email

11 Short for *wireless fidelity*

12 A code of behaviour for online communication, especially in forums, chat rooms and email

Down: a public place where you can pay to use the Internet

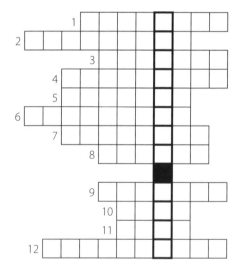

1 mark for each correct answer   **Total __/12**

B Language work

4 Make a question for Tom Morris for each of his answers (1–8). Try to find out the information in bold.

Example: Tom Morris lives in **York**.
Where does he live?

1 He is **32 years old**.
_____

2 He first used the Internet in **1994**.
_____

3 He works as a **webmaster.**
_____

4 He's been doing this job **for two years.**
_____

5 He uses DreamWeaver **to design web pages.**
_____

6 He chats with his family online **twice a week.**
_____

7 He sends emails to **friends and colleagues**.
_____

8 He is subscribed to **three** newsgroups.
_____

1 mark for each correct answer   Total _/8

5 Complete Part I in the history of computers with the past simple of the verbs in brackets.

Part I

2000 BC – The abacus (emerge) _____ in Asia, allowing people to make calculations.

1642 AD – Blaise Pascal (invent) _____ the first mechanical adding machine, the Pascaline.

1941 – Konrad Zuse (build) _____ the first binary digital computer, called Z3.

1969 – The US Dept of Defense (create) _____ ARPANET, the precursor to the Internet.

1971 – Intel (release) _____ the first microprocessor, and Ray Tomlinson (develop) _____ an email program.

1975 – Bill Gates and Paul Allen (found) _____ Microsoft and (write) _____ a BASIC compiler.

1 mark for each correct answer   Total _/8

6 Read Part II in the history of computers and then make questions using the past simple. Answer the questions.

Part II

1981 – IBM sells the first PC.

1984 – Apple develops the Macintosh, the first computer with a graphical user interface.

1991 – Tim Berners-Lee creates the Web at the *Conseil Européen pour la Recherche Nucléaire.*

1995 – CompuServe begins providing internet access.

1999 – MP3 music becomes fashionable.

2001 – Napster lets users download music files, but maintains that it doesn't encourage piracy.

2006 – Hackers steal the credit card numbers of thousands of AT&T customers.

Example: When / IBM / sell / the first PC?
    Q: *When did IBM sell the first PC?*
    A: *IBM sold the first PC in 1981.*

1 What / Apple / do / in 1984?
  Q: _____
  A: _____

2 Who / create / the Web at CERN?
  Q: _____
  A: _____

3 When / MP3 music / become fashionable?
  Q: _____
  A: _____

4 What / happen / in 2001?
  Q: _____
  A: _____

5 What kind of data / hackers / steal from AT&T?
  Q: _____
  A: _____

1 mark for each correct answer   Total _/10

C Reading

7 Read the text and answer these questions.

1 What is the objective of the W3C Consortium?

2 Why is the early Web described as the *read-only Web*?

3 What web phenomena illustrate online collaboration and sharing among users?

4 Which search tool lets you answer questions asked by other people?

5 Which web-based program can help you carry out office tasks?

6 What is the RDF language used for?

7 Which popular site exemplifies the Web as a 3-D environment?

2 marks for each correct answer   Total _/14

Past, present and future of the Web

The Web is constantly evolving. Websites and user preferences change over time, and new online communities are formed every day. To describe the different stages in web evolution, some experts use numbers like Web 1.0, Web 2.0 and Web 3.0.

Web 1.0

The Web was invented by Tim Berners-Lee and Robert Cailliau at CERN in 1991. The former founded the W3C Consortium in 1994 to ensure compatibility between web technologies. This consortium set the standards of the Web as we know it today, including URLs, the HTTP protocol and the HTML language. The early Web contained static information in the form of text, pictures and hyperlinks. It is referred to as the *read-only Web,* because it only allowed users to search for information and read it.

With the arrival of Java in 1995 and web browsers that supported audio and video plug-ins, the Web became more dynamic and interactive, allowing users to play music and video. This was the era of the dial-up modem and the dot-com boom. It was the time of commercial online services, the AltaVista search engine, and webmail with Hotmail.

Web 2.0

This is the current generation of the Web, described as the *read-write Web.*

The Web has become a place of collaboration, citizen journalism and user-generated content. This is exemplified by phenomena such as blogs, collective editing (Wikipedia), video-sharing (YouTube), social networking (Facebook) and social search (Yahoo! Answers). Yahoo! Answers is a site that allows users to ask and answer questions posed by other users. Another example is Flickr, a photo-sharing site that allows users to upload photos and label them with *folksonomies,* keyword tags that help you find images about a certain topic.

A lot of software is executed from scripts embedded in web pages. Two examples are Google Maps, a free maptping service, and ThinkFree Online, a free office suite that runs inside a browser, imitating PC applications such as word processing, spreadsheets and presentations.

Other features of Web 2.0 are the extension of ADSL connections and the emergence of the mobile Internet.

Web 3.0

Web 3.0 might be defined as a third generation of the Web, enabled by the convergence of several trends:

- Fast connections and ubiquitous computing, where users have internet access anytime, anywhere.

- Open-source software and open data; one example is Creative Commons licences, which let people copy and distribute the work under certain conditions.

- Applications hosted on the Web and operated via voice and hand or eye gestures.

- The Semantic Web, which uses languages such as RDF (Resource Description Framework) to publish data so that it can be manipulated and understood by *intelligent software agents;* RDF provides a method for classification of data in order to improve searching and navigation.

- The three-dimensional Web, where sites are transformed into 3-D shared spaces, similar to the virtual reality community of Second Life.

8 Find the following in the text.

1   a program that enables you to view web pages

   _____

2   software which finds information on the Web by looking for words which you have typed in

   _____

3   a common term for any web-based email

   _____

4   websites that contain text entries in reverse chronological order about a particular topic

   _____

5   a collaborative website whose content can be edited by its visitors

   _____

6   terms used to categorize web content with tags

   _____

7   software that is freely distributed

   _____

1 mark for each correct answer   **Total __/7**

9 Complete these sentences with words from the box.

search for	online	upload	mobile

1   Commercial _____ services function like ISPs, but also provide their own unique content.
2   Wireless technologies are enabling the next major wave – the _____ Internet.
3   How do I _____ information on the Web?
4   You can _____ photos to Flickr via email.

2 marks for each correct answer   **Total __ / 8**

D Writing

10 Write an essay (80–110 words) about how the Internet could help reduce paper and costs at your school or office. Consider these ideas:

- What type of computers and network do you have?
- How can you scan, edit and distribute printed material?
- What services are offered by the school/company website?
- Who manages the school/company website?
- Do parents / members of the public have access to the site? What for?
- Is it possible for students / workers to upload material from home?
- How many teachers post exercises on the site?
- Can email replace paper faxes?
- Would it be possible to have a paperless school/office in the future?

Total __/18

TOTAL A+B+C+D ____/ 100

A Vocabulary

1 Decide the type of application software (a–h) that these people should use.

1 'I'd like to retouch photos on my computer.' ☐

2 'I work for a company specializing in designing and publishing catalogues and brochures.' ☐

3 'We're an organization that makes maps and 3-D models of the Earth surface.' ☐

4 'I want to produce illustrations and freehand drawings for an encyclopedia.' ☐

5 'I design web pages for a TV company. I usually include frames, cascading style sheets and multimedia elements on my page designs.' ☐

6 'I teach science and I need to prepare slide shows for my lessons.' ☐

7 'I'm an engineer. I need to design the interior and exterior of a sports car.' ☐

8 'I need a program that supports MIDI and includes a wide range of functions – scales, intervals, melody and rhythm.' ☐

a music software
b CAD software
c paint and image-editing program
d DTP software
e presentation software
f drawing program
g HTML editor
h geographic information system

1 mark for each correct answer　　　　**Total _/8**

2 Solve the clues and complete the puzzle.

1 The most common graphics _____ on the Web are .gif, .jpg and .png.

2 To capture sounds in a digital format and play them back, modern PCs contain a _____ card.

3 Text with links, which takes you to other Web pages.

4 The CTP machine that generates the printing plates for a printing press is called a _____ .

5 A CD _____ is a program that extracts music tracks from audio CDs to files on your hard disk.

6 The technique used to play sound and video files as a continuous stream while they're downloading.

7 Compressed music files can be played with an MP3 _____ .

8 _____ uses text, graphics, audio and video as hypertext elements; all the elements are linked together so that you can easily move from one to another.

9 To make a movie on your PC, you need a special video _____ program.

10 Concerts and other events are broadcast over the Web in a process called _____ .

Down: The integration of text, graphics, audio, video and animation in a single application

1 mark for each correct answer　　　　**Total _ / 11**

3 Complete the sentences with words from the box.

| raster graphics | wireframe | filters | attributes |
| vector graphics | rendering | primitives | toolbox |

1 Graphics programs have a _____ that enables you to draw, paint and edit images on the computer.

2 Bitmaps, or _____ , are stored as a series of tiny dots called pixels.

3 _____ are created using mathematical formulas describing shapes, lines and curves. They are used by drawing programs to create images that can be scaled without loss of quality.

4 The basic elements used to construct graphical objects are called _____ ; they include lines, circles, polygons and text.

5 Line objects can have different kinds of _____ , such as thickness, colour, etc.

6 CAD designers often start a project by making a _____ , a drawing showing the edges and vertices of a 3-D model.

7 _____ is the technique used to make a graphic object look realistic, by adding reflection, shadows and highlights.

8 In image-editing programs, _____ are special effects that can be applied to pictures.

2 marks for each correct answer　　　　**Total _/16**

B Language work

4 Correct the mistakes in these sentences.

1 *Compositing* is combine multiple images together to form one final image.

_____

2 You can view the images by click on this button.

_____

3 While computers are very fast at process some kinds of information, they don't have the flexibility of the human brain.

_____

4 *Gnofract 4D* is a program that allows you to create fractals amazing.

_____

5 This is the largest company in the graphic arts Finnish industry.

_____

6 The Toshiba Satellite X205 is a thin fantastic laptop, with a powerful video card for gaming.

_____

2 marks for each correct answer   **Total __/12**

5 Answer these questions using the second conditional.

What would you do … ?

1 if you had a digital video camera?
  If I had … _____

2 if you found a mobile phone on a bus?

_____

3 if you owned the Internet?

_____

4 if you were a very rich man/woman?

_____

2 marks for each correct answer   **Total __/8**

6 Complete these sentences using modal verbs (*can, could, must, may, might, should*). More than one answer may be possible.

1 I _____ use a computer when I was only five years old.
2 We are looking for a webmaster who _____ design, improve and maintain our website.
3 If you want to see animations, you _____ have Flash Player on your system.
4 Before publishing your website, you _____ check that all the links work.
5 You _____ like to include a counter on your home page to show how many times it has been accessed.

2 marks for each correct answer   **Total __/10**

C Reading

7 Read the text and answer these questions.

1 How are e-publications delivered?
2 Which program is required to view LIT e-books?
3 Which publishing method stores a book in digital format until it's ordered and printed?
4 What types of publication are used as a marketing medium?
5 What are the advantages of self-publishing online?
6 What are the possible uses of electronic ink?

3 marks for each correct answer   **Total __/18**

E-publishing is here to stay!

E-publishing involves the creation, storage and distribution of information in electronic form instead of paper. Such information is delivered via e-books, CD/DVD, email or over the Web. Here we describe the most important methods of e-publishing:

eBooks

An e-book is a digital version of a print book. Depending on the e-book format you select, you can read e-books on a computer, PDA, or a dedicated handheld device known as an e-book reader. Popular e-book formats are: the Rocket e-book, the Mobipocket e-book (with a .prc file extension), the Palm e-book (with a .pdb file extension), and the LIT e-book (readable with the Microsoft Reader).
There are also PDF e-books, read with Adobe Acrobat Reader, and HTML e-books, which can be read with a web browser.

Print-on-demand

Print-on-demand allows books to be printed one at a time, on demand. A book is submitted to the publisher electronically and kept as an electronic file until it is ordered. When the book is ordered by a customer, a special machine prints and binds the book.

Email publishing

Email newsletters are informal publications that deliver information to a target audience. They are easy and cheap to set up online. You subscribe to an e-zine or electronic newsletter, and the publisher sends it out to all the subscribers via email on a set schedule. Newsletters and mailing lists are used by many companies to promote their products or services. Media companies also use them to complement their web and print editions.

Web publishing

Many companies use websites to communicate with potential and existing customers, either as an advertising medium or an online shop.
Most print newspapers are developing online editions, which allow them to effectively compete with TV and radio in presenting breaking news as it happens. There are also web-only newspapers, with no connection to hardcopy formats.
Blogs and wikis are two forms of personal publishing in which individuals become active producers of information. Most people use blogs to post their opinions. A wiki is a collaborative website whose content can be edited by its users (e.g. Wikipedia).
RSS is a format for publishing frequently updated content, such as blog entries, news headlines or podcasts. RSS feeds are read with the help of an RSS reader or aggregator. Each time the aggregator checks your subscriptions, it reports back to you on any new content that is available.
Some e-authors choose to self-publish their books. Self-publishing is, of course, much less expensive than getting a book printed. Marketing and distribution costs are lower as well, as this is done via the Web.

Digital libraries

Digital libraries are collections of books, journals and other materials stored in digital format. The digital content may be stored locally, or accessed via the Internet.

CD/DVD publications

Many encyclopedias, dictionaries and training courses are now available on CD/DVD and online. CD/DVD publications have the advantage of being cheaply produced and extremely portable. In addition, they contain links between related content and include media (audio, video and animations), which are impossible to store in the printed format.

Electronic ink

Electronic ink is a special type of ink that can display different colours when exposed to an electric field. E-ink is ideal for Electronic Paper Displays (EPDs). Applications include billboards that rotate different ads, coupons that update themselves with the latest offer, T-shirts displaying different messages, books and newspapers that update themselves, etc.

E Ink Corporation and Xerox are two companies that are currently developing this technology.

8 Find the following in the text.

1   the electronic counterpart of a print book _____

2   a file format that requires the Acrobat Reader _____

3   user-generated sites that display posting in chronological order _____

4   a site that can be edited by its visitors _____

5   an organized collection of digital documents _____

1 mark for each correct answer   **Total _/5**

D Writing

9 Read these posts from a message thread called *E-books versus paper books*. Add your response, giving your opinion on the topic.

I am open to all new technologies, but I still prefer books the old way. I have a book collection at home and I like the feel and smell of paper books. E-books don't have the charm of books that you can touch and read. I also enjoy buying and lending books to my friends.

However, e-books could be a good solution for some people who have trouble reading. Personally, I feel that print books will never go out of fashion; e-books will simply complement the hardcopy versions.

Posted by Nicole, January 15th at 10:15

I guess e-books will never completely replace the real thing, but they have a lot of advantages: they're cheaper than paper versions (no printing or distribution costs); I can download e-books instantly and store hundreds on one device; paper books, however, take up a lot of space.

I really like e-books. I can have bookmarks, search text, use links, etc. These features are really useful when talking about reference works.

A final detail: e-books are environmentally friendly – no trees have to be cut down to create them.

Posted by Ryan, January 20th at 3:20 pm

Submit comment:

_____
_____
_____
_____
_____
_____
_____
_____

Total _/12

TOTAL A+B+C+D ___/ 100

A Vocabulary

1 Complete the text with words from the box.

flowchart	program	bugs	coding	debugging
documentation	compiled			

Programming steps

To write a (1) _____ , software engineers usually follow these steps:

First of all, they try to understand exactly what the problem is and decide, in a general way, how to solve it.

The next phase is to design a step-by-step plan of instructions. This usually takes the form of a (2) _____ , a diagram that uses special symbols showing the logical relationship between the parts of the program.

Next they write the instructions in a high-level computer language like PASCAL, COBOL, or C++. This is called (3) _____ . The program is then (4) _____ , a process that converts the source code into machine code.

When the program is written, they have to test it with sample data to see if there are (5)_____ , or errors. The process of correcting these errors is called (6) _____ . Software developers conduct a series of tests until the program runs smoothly.

Finally, they write detailed (7) _____ for users. Manuals tell us how to use the programs.

2 marks for each correct answer **Total __/14**

2 Complete these sentences using the correct form of the word in brackets. You will need to add a suffix to each word.

1 Pascal is used in universities to teach the fundamentals of _____ . (program)

2 A _____ translates the source code into object code – i.e. it converts the entire program into machine code in one go. (compile)

3 Visual BASIC enables _____ to create all sorts of Windows applications. (program)

4 Voice XML is a programming language created in 2000 to make web content _____ via the telephone. (access)

5 C is widely used to write system software and _____ applications. (commerce)

1 mark for each correct answer **Total _ / 5**

3 Complete these sentences with the jobs from the box.

webmaster	blog administrator	hardware engineer
help desk technician	network administrator	
computer security specialist		

1 A computer _____ is responsible for designing and developing the electronic and mechanical parts of computers.

2 A _____ has access to the blog settings and has the ability to edit and remove posts made by other members.

3 A _____ manages a LAN within an organization.

4 A _____ regulates access to computer data and prevents unauthorized modification or destruction of information.

5 A _____ provides phone or email support on technical issues, including operation of equipment, setup problems, troubleshooting, etc.

6 A _____ must be proficient in HTML, XML and JavaScript.

1 mark for each correct answer **Total __/6**

B Language work

4 Choose the correct answer (a–c) to complete the sentences.

1 It's important _____ programming languages with markup languages.
   a not confuse   **b** not to confuse   **c** don't confuse

2 Markup languages are used _____ the structure of web documents.
   a for describe   **b** describe   **c** to describe

3 You must learn _____ effective business letters.
   a to write   **b** write   **c** writing

4 Mr Keller has asked me _____ you these files.
   a send   **b** sending   **c** to send

5 This program will make this old PC _____ faster.
   a running   **b** run   **c** to run

1 mark for each correct answer **Total __/5**

5 Look at the list and write sentences describing what Kelly did or didn't do last week.

Example: *On Monday she began a course on Java; she didn't phone her parents*

Mon begin a course on Java ✓
phone parents ✗

Tue write an e-mail to Andy ✓
watch TV ✗

1 _____
_____

Wed repair the printer ✗
visit Jane in hospital ✓

2 _____
_____

Thu read the *Financial Times* ✗
send an e-card to Ibrahim in Egypt ✓

3 _____
_____

Fri have lunch with my boss ✓
go to my German class ✗

4 _____
_____

Sat buy a portable DVD drive for my brother ✓
5 _____

Sun download some music from the Net ✓
6 _____

1 mark for each correct answer   **Total _ /10**

6 Put the verbs into the present perfect simple or past simple.

1 IBM (develop) _____ Fortran in the mid-1950s to create scientific and engineering applications.
2 John (be) _____ a software engineer since May 2006.
3 Once I (realize) _____ that I had a virus, I ran my virus protection program.
4 (you ever work) _____ as a web designer?

2 marks for each correct answer   **Total _ /8**

7 Put the verbs into the present perfect simple or continuous.

1 John (surf) _____ the Web since 2000, and everyday he finds new things that catch his eye.
2 I have (apply) _____ for several jobs in recent months.
3 How many emails (you receive) _____ so far today?
4 I (look) _____ at the screen for too long. Now my eyes are sore and tired.

2 marks for each correct answer   **Total _ /8**

C Reading

8 Read this job advertisement and write three important requirements for the job.

GRAPHIC DESIGNER

www.ajastakeyhtio.fi

We are seeking a self-motivated graphic designer with experience in design and layout for print media. The position requires extensive experience with the Adobe Creative Suite – Illustrator, InDesign, Photoshop, Flash and Acrobat.

The candidate should be familiar with both PC and Mac platforms. Skills in web design are desirable. Must be able to work in a team.

Send your CV and samples of work to: Ari Mikkola, Personnel Manager, Ajasta Keyhtio Publishing, Mäkituvantie, 27, Helsinki

---

1 _____
2 _____
3 _____

2 marks for each correct answer   **Total _ /6**

9 Read the letter of application on the following page and answer these questions.

1 How did Eva Neumann find out about the job?

_____

2 Where did she do her practical training?

_____

3 How long has she been working at VEM Verlag?

_____

4 Why does she want to change jobs?

_____

5 What is the earliest date she could start working?

_____

2 marks for each correct answer   **Total _ /10**

Dasselstr 28
50674 Köln
Germany
3rd March 2008

Mr Mikkola
Ajasta Keyhtio Publishing
Mäkituvantie 27,
Helsinki

Dear Mr Mikkola,

I am writing to apply for the job of graphic designer, which was advertised on your company website.

I have a bachelor's degree in graphic design from Köln Technical College, Germany. I started to work in the DTP field six years (1) _____ , when I attended an in-company training course in Helsinki as part of the Leonardo Da Vinci Program. The project was coordinated by Heltech College, and I did practical training in Lönberg P.O., a Finnish company specializing in printing advertising material.

Before taking my present job, I worked for two years with KBI, a German publishing company, where I used Adobe Illustrator, Photoshop and QuarkXpress to lay out books and magazines. I stayed in this job (2) _____ June 2004.

(3) _____ the last three years I have been working part-time at VEM Verlag, where I've been responsible for visual graphic design and digital imaging. (4) _____ February this year I have been using Adobe InDesign, the new standard in professional page layout. I have knowledge of mainstream computer platforms, including Macintosh and Windows.

I would welcome the opportunity to work for your company. I would like to improve my graphic and typographic design skills and eventually move into management.

Please find enclosed my CV along with samples of my work. I will be available for an interview at any time. The earliest date that I could start work is 21 May.

I look forward to hearing from you.

Yours sincerely,

Eva Neumann

Eva Neumann

10 Complete the letter with *for, since, ago* and *until*.

2 marks for each correct answer   Total _/8

D Writing

11 Angela Rusell is interested in the job of Computer Sales Assistant, as advertised below. Use the notes for her CV to write a letter applying for the job.

COMPUTER SALES ASSISTANT

This is a good opportunity to work for **PC Market**, the largest computer shop in the city. You must have some knowledge of operating systems and peripherals.

You will help the Sales Manager to install all kinds of software and to sell computer products. Some experience in customer relations may be useful. Driving licence essential.

Send your CV to PC Market,
27 Castle Street, Cardiff CD2 3BA
Phone: 0362 698385
E-mail: barnett@pcmarketmail.net

Notes for CV

Education:
- Three A levels and a one-year diploma in IT

Qualifications:
- Knowledge of Windows, Mac OS and Linux
- Familiar with a wide range of programs, e.g. MS Office

Work experience:
- Employed for two years as a data entry operator
- Experience in installing and testing PCs and peripherals

Other details:
- Hobbies: web surfing, music, travelling
- Driving licence and car
- Good with people

Total _ / 20

TOTAL A+B+C+D ___/ 100

A Vocabulary

1 Choose the correct answers.

1 This type of network links computers in a small area, such as a single room or building.
   a LAN   **b** MAN   **c** WAN

2 On this network topology, all devices are connected to a central hub, or station, which redistributes the data.
   a bus   **b** star   **c** ring

3 This device connects your computer or home network to the Internet.
   a ADSL port   **b** Ethernet   **c** modem-router

4 The wireless technology that allows handheld devices and mobile phones to communicate over short distances is called
   a Wi-Fi   **b** Bluetooth   **c** Wireless LAN

5 The Internet uses the _____ protocol to transfer information.
   a TCP/IP   **b** USB   **c** ADSL

6 This is the geographic boundary covered by a Wi-Fi wireless access point.
   a wireless router   **b** WiMAX zone   **c** hotspot

1 mark for each correct answer   **Total __/6**

2 Write two words with each of these suffixes.

1 tele- _____

_____

2 trans- _____

_____

3 inter- _____

_____

4 cyber- _____

_____

2 marks for each correct answer   **Total __/8**

3 Complete these sentences with words from the box.

| multiplayer | console games | game platform |
| game genre | arcade games | PC games |

1 The four major types of _____ are PCs, consoles, handhelds and the Internet.

2 _____ are played on a personal computer connected to a high-resolution monitor.

3 You play _____ on machines like the Xbox.

4 Some games have a _____ facility that allows lots of people to play the same game at the same time.

5 A Role-playing game (RPG) is a _____ where the participants adopt a role, represented by their character, or avatar.

6 Most _____ are video games or pinball machines controlled by joysticks, buttons, steering wheels and foot pedals.

1 mark for each correct answer   **Total __/6**

4 Match the technologies (1–7) with the descriptions (a–g).

1 Nanotechnology ☐
2 Artificial Intelligence ☐
3 RFID ☐
4 GPS ☐
5 Biometrics ☐
6 VoIP ☐
7 Digital TV ☐

a biological identification of people

b a service which allows users to make phone calls over the Internet

c the science of making small devices from single atoms and molecules

d a system for broadcasting and receiving moving pictures and sound by means of digital signals

e a navigation and location system formed by various satellites and their corresponding receivers on Earth

f the study of methods by which a computer can simulate aspects of human intelligence

g the use of radio waves and chip-equipped tags to automatically identify people or things

1 mark for each correct answer   **Total __/7**

B Language work

5 Complete these texts with the passive form of the verbs in brackets. Be sure to use the correct tense.

> **Sound and music**
>
> The Phonograph (1) _____ (invent) by Thomas Edison in 1877, who discovered how to record music and voice on a metal cylinder of tin foil. Ten years later, Emile Berlinger invented a method of reproducing sound on rotating discs with a spiral groove – the first gramophone records.
>
> Magnetic tapes (2) _____ (manufacture) by German audio engineers at AEG and Bash in the 1930s, and the first compact disc (3) _____ (design) by Philips and Sony in 1980. Three years later, CDs reached the market in Asia and the US. In the near future, CDs (4) _____ (probably replace) by new technologies such DVD-Audio, HD-DVD and Blu-ray discs.
>
> The most recent development in digital recording has been the MP3 format, which has generated the market for portable MP3 players and iPods. Today, more than 50% of all music (5) _____ (buy) online and many music tracks (6) _____ (download) illegally.

The telephone

Alexander Graham Bell is remembered today as the inventor of the telephone in 1876. A year later, his invention (7) _____ (improve) by Thomas Edison, by adding a microphone.

The first fully automatic mobile phone (8) _____ (introduce) by Motorola in 1981. Nowadays, new mobile phones (9) _____ (develop), with emphasis on multimedia, radio and real-time TV. Some models (10) _____ (call) smartphones.

The computer

The first computers built using silicon chips went on sale in 1965. Microsoft (11) _____ (found) by Bill Gates and Paul Allen in 1975 to sell a version of the BASIC language for the Altair computer. The first IBM-PC (12) _____ (sell) in 1981, becoming a standard for personal computers.

Every year, more and more people get on the Internet. Today, the Web (13) _____ (can access) from PDAs, mobile phones – indeed, from anywhere at any time. In the future, artificial intelligence and voice recognition (14) _____ (incorporate) into most computer applications.

1 mark for each correct answer **Total _/14**

6 Complete these sentences with the correct form of the verbs from the box.

| set up | log on | look up | consist of | make up |
| break into |

1 New mobile phones can be used to _____ to the Internet.
2 If you intend to _____ a wireless LAN, you will need a wireless router.
3 A network _____ two or more computers that are connected together to share information.
4 A hacker _____ the campus computer system last Monday and students were unable to use the Internet.
5 You can use an online Thesaurus to _____ synonyms, antonyms and brief definitions of words.
6 Millions of people share their thoughts and dreams on the wires and computers that _____ the Internet.

1 mark for each correct answer **Total _/6**

7 Complete these sentences with the adverbial form of the words in brackets.

1 Our e-zine is published (month) _____ and is available in PDF file format.
2 PDAs are (wide) _____ used by businessmen and students around the world.
3 CPU speed is a major factor in determining how (fast) _____ your computer operates.

4 E-commerce has become (increasing) _____ popular over the last decade.
5 Not all graphics cards are equal in terms of performance; some will play games (good) _____ and some won't.

1 mark for each correct answer **Total _/5**

8 Correct the mistakes in these sentences.

1 Tiny computers will be embed in our clothes, and even in our bodies.

_____

2 He says he won't has finished the report by Thursday.

_____

3 Some day, we'll be talk to our PC naturally, like we do with friends.

_____

4 In the near future, most PCs will to communicate with other devices without cables.

_____

2 marks for each correct answer **Total _/8**

C Reading

9 Read the text on the following page and write at least four tasks that robots and androids do or might do in the future.

_____
_____
_____
_____
_____
_____
_____

2 marks for each correct answer **Total _ /8**

Robots and androids

Engineers are trying to make computers think and behave like humans. By combining Artificial Intelligence and engineering techniques, they are building many different types of robot and android.

Robots are devices that move and react to sensory input. They usually contain software that runs automatically, without the intervention of a person. Today, robots are used in a wide variety of contexts, from factories to space exploration. We drive cars that have been welded by industrial robots; we buy products that have been made and packaged by robots in an assembly line; we use machines that have been built by robots.

Our life is affected by robotics in many other ways. Just think about medicine and the health system. Tiny computers are used to monitor the heart rate and blood pressure; micro-machines and insect-sized robots help doctors in heart operations and other complicated surgery. In the future, tiny robotic creatures, called nanobots, will be injected into the human body and move through the arteries, curing illnesses.

Robots are also used in dangerous situations – for example, in repairing nuclear plants, cleaning toxic waste and defusing bombs. Robotics has also been incorporated into the first *smart homes*, where there are gadgets that regulate the central heating, sensors that control the solar panels, robot maids that do the housework, etc.

Some research centres are even building androids – robots that have the shape and capabilities of a human being. In the near future, androids will be available for sale. They will have access to the Internet, be a guide for the blind, assist elderly people at home; they could even be a 24-hour security guard for your home, sounding the alarm in case of fire and phoning the police if there is a burglary.

10 Find words in the text with the following meanings.

1 the stage of mass production in which parts of a product move along for progressive assembly _____
2 the study and use of robots _____
3 microscopic cell-sized robots _____
4 buildings where the systems are interconnected to allow automatic and remote control _____
5 devices that receive and respond to a signal or stimulus _____
6 robots that look like human beings _____

2 marks for each correct answer   **Total _/12**

D Writing

11 How do you think developments in ICT will affect these areas of life in the next 20 years? Write a short paragraph for each of these topics, giving your predictions.

1 Intelligent homes
   Example: *We will be able to control our homes from our car, or from a website thousands of miles away.*

   _____

   _____

   _____

2 Health

   _____

   _____

   _____

3 Fashion and clothes

   _____

   _____

   _____

4 Cars

   _____

   _____

   _____

5 Tourism

   _____

   _____

   _____

   _____

Total _ / 20

TOTAL A+B+C+D ___ / 100

Module 1

1

1c 2a 3d 4e 5f 6b

2

1 keep records
2 make video calls
3 access the Internet
4 dispense money
5 store information
6 download ringtones

3

1f 2e 3d 4a 5c 6b

4

1 The CPU is a chip which/that acts as the brain of a computer.
2 A hacker is a person who/that invades a network's privacy.
3 A modem is an electronic device which/that enables a computer to communicate with another over telephone lines.
4 A software engineer is someone who writes computer programs.
5 The mobile phone is a device which/that people use for communicating with each other.

5

1e 2b 3g 4d 5f 6a 7c

6

1 Do you need any help?
2 we're looking for a portable computer
3 They are both very fast
4 What's the storage capacity of the hard disk?
5 has a 15.4" LCD screen
6 how much do they cost?
7 you're obviously getting a faster computer, with more memory

7

1 A PDA usually runs on batteries.
2 A touch-sensitive LCD screen
3 If the device doesn't incorporate handwriting recognition, you use the stylus to tap on the letters of a miniature on-screen keyboard.

4 Windows Mobile, Palm OS, RIM (for BlackBerry wireless devices), Symbian OS (for Nokia or Samsung smartphones)
5 With a PDA, you can manage personal information, such as contacts, appointments and to-do lists. You can play games, record voice and video, and connect to the Internet. You can also use it as a radio, MP3 player and GPS device.
6 PDA processors are smaller, cheaper and less powerful than those in standard PCs. PDAs don't have a hard disk.
7 To synchronize and transfer data between a PDA and a standard PC, you need to connect the devices via a USB cable or wirelessly (with IrDA or Bluetooth wireless technologies).

8

1 stylus
2 speech recognition system
3 smartphone
4 GPS
5 RISC (reduced instruction set computer)
6 flash memory
7 wireless

9

Open task

Module 2

1

1b 2f 3d 4a 5g 6h
7c 8e

2

1 manufacturer
2 technology
3 brightness
4 wireless
5 colourful
6 photographic
7 innovative

3

1 magnifier
2 Braille

3 textphone
4 widescreen
5 pixels
6 ergonomics

4

1 Liquid Crystal Display
2 Cathode Ray Tube
3 Repetitive Strain Injury
4 Dots Per Inch
5 Web Accessibility Initiative
6 Universal Serial Bus

5 Possible answers

1 A printer is an output device which prints out text or graphics on paper.
2 A touch screen is a touch-sensitive display which lets you use your finger to point directly at objects on the screen.
3 A game controller is an input device connected to a game console or a PC, used to control a video game.

6

1 faster; cheaper
2 more powerful; most advanced
3 highest
4 heavier
5 worst
6 more expensive
7 least reliable

7

1 A system that recognizes speech
2 A computer that is activated by voice
3 The laptop that belongs to the teacher
4 A program that is used to draw and paint

8

1 graphical user interface, or GUI
2 computer simulation
3 data glove (or VR glove)
4 motion detectors
5 flight simulators
6 remotely operated robots

9

1 virtual reality
2 virtual interface

3 head-mounted display (HMD)
4 stereoscopic vision
5 joystick
6 tiny

10

Open task

Module 3

1

1f   2b   3a   4e   5d   6g   7c

2

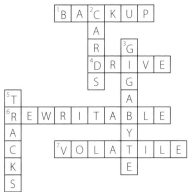

3

1 shouldn't   3 should
2 –   4 shouldn't

4

1 As a result
2 whereas
3 because
4 Although

5

1 computerize
2 digitally
3 magnetized
4 fragmented
5 blogosphere
6 handheld
7 wireless

6

a 3
b 1
c 2

7

1 The average access time of the SpinPoint F1drive is 8.9 ms.
2 Perpendicular Magnetic Recording (PMR)

3 Flash memory is used as a non-volatile disk cache, a mechanism that allows quick access to data so data can be retrieved faster, reducing the use of the hard disk and cutting power consumption.
4 Samsung released the R55, the first computer with a hybrid hard drive
5 It's called Blu-ray because it uses a blue-violet laser
6 A dual layer Blu-ray disc can store 50GB.

8

1 terabyte
2 platters
3 disk utilities
4 hybrid hard drive
5 disk cache
6 laser
7 backward compatible

9

Open task

Module 4

1

1b   2g   3a   4e   5d   6h
7f   8c

2

1c   2d   3a   4g   5b   6e   7f

3

1d   2f   3a   4c   5g   6h
7e   8b

4

1 column
2 row
3 cell
4 formulae
5 record
6 field
7 query

5

1 **some** advice
2 information**s is**
3 **a lot of / many** Windows versions
4 homework**s**
5 **a little** time

6

1 the   6 –
2 –   7 an
3 –   8 –
4 an   9 –
5 a   10 the

7

1 businesses
2 software
3 technologies
4 analyses
5 taxes
6 switches
7 women
8 children
9 formulae/formulas
10 queries

8

1 First, find the picture that you want to insert as an illustration in a Word document.
2 Move your cursor over the picture and right click. A pop up menu will appear on the screen. Choose *Copy* to copy the image onto the Clipboard.
3 Next, switch to your Word document and click where you want to insert the image.
4 Then choose *Edit* on the Menu bar at the top of the screen, and click *Paste*. This will insert the picture at the insertion point.
5 Once the picture has been pasted, you may like to resize it and move it to a different location.

9

1 False – An **office** suite lets you create documents, …
2 True
3 False – **OpenOffice** is free to …
4 True

10

1 Office suites usually combine a word processor, a spreadsheet program and a presentation program, but they can also contain a database manager, an email client, a web browser, Instant Messaging, collaboration groupware, and a personal information manager, or PIM.
2 *OpenOffice* is a free, open-source suite, so anyone can use it or modify it.
3 The components of an office suite share a consistent graphical user interface.
4 Some office suites include a document recovery tool that helps you retrieve documents after a system failure.

11

1 office suite
2 productivity suite
3 collaboration groupware
4 relational database
5 OLE (object linking and embedding)
6 operating system

12

Open task

Module 5

1

1b　2a　3c　4c　5b　6b　7a

2

1b　2g　3a　4c　5h　6e
7d　8f

3

	1	e	m	o	t	i	c	o	n		
2	h	y	p	e	r	l	i	n	k		
		3	y	o	u	t	u	b	e		
	4	e	-	c	o	m	m	e	r	c	e
	5	m	a	l	w	a	r	e			
6	b	r	o	a	d	b	a	n	d			
	7	c	r	a	c	k	e	r	s		
	8	a	v	a	t	a	r				
	9	p	o	d	c	a	s	t			
	10	s	p	a	m						
	11	W	i	F	i						
12	n	e	t	i	q	u	e	t	t	e		

4

1 How old is he?
2 When did he first use the Internet?
3 What is his job? / What does he do?
4 How long has he been doing this job?
5 What does he use *DreamWeaver* for?
6 How often does he chat with his family online?
7 Who does he send email to?
8 How many newsgroups is he subscribed to?

5

2000 BC	emerged
1642 AD	invented
1941	built
1969	created
1971	released; developed
1975	founded; wrote

6

1 Q: What did Apple do in 1984?
A: Apple developed the Macintosh, the first computer with a GUI.
2 Q: Who created the Web at CERN?
A: Tim Berners-Lee created the Web.
3 Q: When did MP3 music become fashionable?
A: MP3 music became fashionable in 1999.
4 Q: What happened in 2001?
A: Napster let users download music files, but maintained that it didn't encourage piracy.
5 Q: What kind of data did hackers steal from AT&T?
A: Hackers stole the credit card numbers of thousands of AT&T customers.

7

1 The objective of the W3C consortium is to ensure compatibility between web technologies.
2 Because it only allowed users to search for information and read it.
3 Online collaboration and sharing is exemplified by web phenomena such as blogs, collective editing (Wikipedia), video-sharing (YouTube), photo-sharing (Flickr), social networking (Facebook) and social search (Yahoo! Answers).
4 Yahoo! Answers
5 ThinkFree Online

6 The RDF language is used for classification of data in order to improve web searching and navigation.
7 Second Life exemplifies the Web as a 3-D environment.

8

1 web browser
2 search engine
3 webmail
4 blogs
5 Wikipedia
6 folksonomies
7 open-source software

9

1 online
2 mobile
3 search for
4 upload

10

Open task

Module 6

1

1c　2d　3h　4f　5g　6e
7b　8a

2

				1	f	o	r	m	a	t	s
			2	s	o	u	n	d			
		3	h	y	p	e	r	l	i	n	k	
4	p	l	a	t	e	s	e	t	t	e	r	
					5	r	i	p	p	e	r
		6	s	t	r	e	a	m	i	n	g	
			7	p	l	a	y	e	r		
8	h	y	p	e	r	m	e	d	i	a			
			9	e	d	i	t	i	n	g	
		10	w	e	b	c	a	s	t		

3

1 toolbox
2 raster graphics
3 Vector graphics
4 primitives
5 attributes
6 wireframe
7 Rendering
8 filters

4

1 … is combin**ing**
2 … by click**ing**
3 … at process**ing**
4 … **amazing fractals**

5 ... **Finnish graphics arts industry**
6 ... a **fantastic, thin** laptop

5 Possible answers

1 If I had a digital video camera, I'd make a video clip and post it on YouTube.
2 If I found a mobile phone on a bus, I'd give it to the bus driver.
3 If I owned the Internet, I'd ban indecent material.
4 If I were a very rich man or woman, I'd buy computers for poor children.

6

1 could
2 can
3 must
4 should/must
5 may/might

7

1 E-publications are delivered via ebooks, CD/DVD, email, or over the Web.
2 The Microsoft Reader
3 Print on-demand
4 Newsletters and mailing lists
5 Self-publishing online is much less expensive than getting a book printed. Marketing and distribution costs are lower as well.
6 Applications of electronic ink include billboards that rotate different ads, offer coupons that update themselves with the latest offer, T-shirts displaying different messages, books and newspapers that update themselves, etc.

8

1 e-book
2 .pdf
3 blogs
4 wiki
5 digital library

9 Open task

Module 7

1

1 program
2 flowchart
3 coding
4 compiled
5 bugs
6 debugging
7 documentation

2

1 programming
2 compiler
3 programmers
4 accessible
5 commercial

3

1 hardware engineer
2 blog administrator
3 network administrator
4 computer security specialist
5 help desk technician
6 webmaster

4

1b   2c   3a   4c   5b

5

On Tuesday she wrote an email to Andy; she didn't watch TV.

On Wednesday she didn't repair the printer; she visited Jane in hospital.

On Thursday she didn't read the *Financial Times*; she sent an e-card to Ibrahim in Egypt.

On Friday she had lunch with her boss; she didn't go to her German class.

On Saturday she bought a portable DVD drive for her brother.

On Sunday she downloaded some music from the Net.

6

1 developed
2 has been
3 realized
4 Have you ever worked

7

1 has been surfing
2 have applied
3 have you received
4 have been looking

8

The candidate should have extensive experience with Adobe Creative Suite – Illustrator, InDesign, Photoshop, Flash and Acrobat; be familiar with both PC and Mac platforms; be able to work in a team.

9

1 She saw the job advertisement on the company website.
2 She did her practical training in Lönberg P.O. (a Finnish company specializing in printing advertising material), as part of the Leonardo da Vinci program.
3 She has been working at VEM Verlag for the last three years.
4 She wants to improve her graphic and typographic design skills, and move into management.
5 The earliest date she could start work is 21 May.

10

1 ago
2 until
3 For
4 Since

11 Open task

Module 8

1

1a   2b   3c   4b   5a   6c

2 Possible answers

1 telecommunications, teleworking
2 transmission, transaction
3 Internet, interconnect
4 cybercafé, cyberspace

3

1 game platform
2 PC games
3 console games
4 multiplayer
5 game genre
6 arcade games

4

1c   2f   3g   4e   5a   6b   7d

5

1 was invented
2 were manufactured
3 was designed
4 will probably be replaced
5 is bought
6 are downloaded
7 was improved
8 was introduced
9 are being developed
10 are called
11 was founded
12 was sold
13 can be accessed
14 will be incorporated

6

1 log on
2 set up
3 consists of
4 broke into
5 look up
6 make up

7

1 monthly
2 widely
3 fast
4 increasingly
5 well

8

1 will be embedd**ed**
2 won't ha**ve** finished
3 we'll be talk**ing**
4 **will** communicate

9   Possible answers

- Industrial robots are used to weld cars, make and package products, and build machines.
- Micro-machines and insect-sized robots are used to monitor the heart rate and blood pressure and to help doctors in heart operations and surgery.
- Nanobots will be injected into the human body and cure illnesses.
- Robots are used in dangerous situations – for example, to repair nuclear plants, clean toxic waste, and defuse bombs.
- Androids will be used to access the Internet, guide the blind, assist elderly people, act as a security guard, etc.

10

1 assembly line
2 robotics
3 nanobots
4 smart homes
5 sensors
6 androids

11 Open task